CHURCH HURT

Copyright © 2025 by André Butler

Published by AVAIL

All rights reserved. No portion of this book may be reproduced, stored in a retrieval system, or transmitted in any form or by any means—electronic, mechanical, photocopy, recording, scanning, or other—except for brief quotations in critical reviews or articles, without prior written permission of the author.

Unless otherwise specified, all Scripture quotations are taken from the Holy Bible, New Living Translation, copyright © 1996, 2004, 2015 by Tyndale House Foundation. Used by permission of Tyndale House Publishers, Inc., Carol Stream, Illinois 60188. All rights reserved. | Scripture quotations marked AMPC are taken from the Amplified® Bible, Classic Edition, Copyright © 1954, 1958, 1962, 1964, 1965, 1987 by The Lockman Foundation. | Scripture quotations marked BBE are taken from the 1949/1964 Bible in Basic English, public domain. | Scripture quotations marked KJV are taken from the King James Version of the Bible. Public domain. | Scripture quotations marked MSG are taken from THE MESSAGE, copyright © 1993, 1994, 1995, 1996, 2000, 2001, 2002 by Eugene H. Peterson. Used by permission of NavPress. All rights reserved. Represented by Tyndale House Publishers, Inc. | Scripture quotations marked NIV are taken from the Holy Bible, New International Version®, NIV®. Copyright © 1973, 1978, 1984, 2011 by Biblica, Inc.™ Used by permission of Zondervan. All rights reserved worldwide. www.zondervan.com. The "NIV" and "New International Version" are trademarks registered in the United States Patent and Trademark Office by Biblica, Inc.™ | Scripture quotations marked NKJV are taken from the New King James Version®. Copyright © 1982 by Thomas Nelson. Used by permission. All rights reserved.

For foreign and subsidiary rights, contact the author.

Cover design by: Sara Young
Cover photo by: Kai Davis

ISBN: 978-1-964794-89-1   1 2 3 4 5 6 7 8 9 10

Printed in the United States of America

PRAISE FOR
CHURCH HURT

I have a saying that goes, "Don't fold while you're still unfolding," and that is the crux of the message in *Church Hurt*. André Butler did an amazing job walking us all through the mess of being hurt by the church, and teaches us how to turn that into our message. *Church Hurt* is for anyone who has ever experienced hurt in the church world, and this message could not come at a better time.

—TIM STOREY
Thought leader, life strategist, author, speaker, and counselor

Church Hurt by Pastor André Butler speaks right to the heart of a pain that too many of us know but often struggle to overcome. In this powerful book, Pastor André skillfully unveils how God's healing can truly restore our spirits, lifting us beyond the hurt and into the freedom and joy He intended. If you've felt betrayed, disappointed, or let down by the church, this book is a must-read. It's time to let God work in you and experience the future He has for you, free from the enemy's tactics that keep you bound. Let your healing begin here.

—HEATHER LINDSEY
Author and entrepreneur

Pastor André Butler's *Church Hurt* is a timely and much-needed resource for the body of Christ. For anyone who has experienced pain in the church, this book offers powerful wisdom, understanding, and a clear path to healing and restoration. I also recommend this book to church leadership and attendees, as its insights not only help those currently facing church hurt but also prepare and equip readers to navigate or support others in similar situations. It's a great and much-needed resource for these times.

—MICHELLE FERGUSON
MiChelle Ferguson Ministries

André Butler's *Church Hurt: It's Time to Heal* speaks directly to those who have been wounded by the very place they once turned to for hope and connection. With empathy and spiritual insight, Butler unpacks the complexities of "church hurt," guiding readers to understand its roots, recognize God's heart for their healing, and take tangible steps toward wholeness. This book does more than address the pain; it empowers readers to see beyond past disappointments and embrace a renewed relationship with God and His Church. Church Hurt is a vital read for anyone ready to experience true spiritual healing and re-engage with their faith community with confidence and peace.

—GEORGE DAVIS
Author and Senior Pastor
Impact Church

CHURCH HURT

IT'S TIME TO HEAL

ANDRÉ BUTLER

CONTENTS

INTRODUCTION 9
CHAPTER 1. CHURCH HURT HURTS 11
CHAPTER 2. MY HEALING STORY 15
CHAPTER 3. IS CHURCH HURT A NEW PHENOMENON? 23
CHAPTER 4. WHO'S BEHIND CHURCH HURT? 29
CHAPTER 5. GOD CARES 37
CHAPTER 6. LET GOD HEAL YOU 45
CHAPTER 7. LET IT GO! 51
CHAPTER 8. DON'T PICK THE SCAB 55
CHAPTER 9. TIME TO GROW 61
CHAPTER 10. THE CHURCH IS FULL OF HYPOCRITES! 71
CHAPTER 11. THE YELLOW BRICK ROAD 79
CHAPTER 12. IS CHURCH REALLY NECESSARY? 85
CHAPTER 13. IS CHURCH ATTENDANCE OPTIONAL? 93
CHAPTER 14. I DON'T NEED A LEADER 103
CHAPTER 15. IT HAPPENS 113
CHAPTER 16. FRIENDLY FIRE 119
CHAPTER 17. CHURCH ISN'T WACK 131
CHAPTER 18. FOR PASTORS ONLY 147
CHAPTER 19. CHURCH HURT AND PREACHERS' KIDS 163
CHAPTER 20. CHURCH HURT AND FAMILY MINISTRY 173
CHAPTER 21. WHEN A LEADER FAILS 187
CHAPTER 22. IT'S TIME TO MOVE PAST CHURCH HURT 193

ABOUT THE AUTHOR 195
ADDITIONAL RESOURCES 197

INTRODUCTION

"The institution of church is wack. I think how the church is run is wack. I think the religious system and structure is wack."

I ran across a video online where a minister I greatly respect used these words to talk about what most people call church. Although I greatly respect the minister and his ministry (in fact, God has used his music to encourage me during some really dark moments), I struggled with these words about the institution of the church. Why did I feel this way about the video I had just seen? I realized that part of the reason it bothered me so much is that so many others think the same way. So many have a real problem with the church. I think the reason for that can be summed up in two words—church hurt.

Many people have been hurt at church or by church. Whether it's through church leadership, members, or beliefs, we've suffered emotional harm in the very place we often go to for emotional healing. Our reaction to that hurt has not always been what God intended. In fact, Satan, God's enemy, has used church hurt to drive many away from their relationships with God and His people. It's time we dealt with this issue once and for all. That's why I wrote this book.

If church hurt is an issue for you, I ask you to dive into this topic with me. If you know someone suffering from church hurt, ask them to read this book along with you. I believe this book is going to help you; it's going to free you to fully experience the future that God has for you!

CHAPTER 1
CHURCH HURT HURTS

Almost everyone who has regularly attended church has at one time or another suffered church hurt.

Church hurt is emotional distress or harm attributed to the institution of the church. It is generally the result of being mistreated by church people or church leadership. You may have experienced church hurt when someone lied to you, cussed you out, gossiped about you, or didn't value or treat you properly. Maybe someone wasn't there for you when you needed them to be there for you. Maybe you had spiritual leadership that had some type of moral failure. Whatever the cause, church hurt HURTS!

You may be asking yourself, "Do I really want to read what a pastor has to say about church hurt?" I get it. You may think that I don't know anything about it, or worse, that I am the cause of it. Let me assure you, I am supremely qualified to write about church hurt. Why do I say that? Let me tell you a little about myself.

I grew up a preacher's kid, also known as a PK. What do you think of when you think about preachers' kids? Many people immediately think about someone who hates church, has run away from church, and lives their life in a completely different way than what churches teach. Why have so many preachers' kids done that? Church hurt.

SOMETIMES, PEOPLE DON'T REALIZE THAT CHURCH LEADERS ALSO EXPERIENCE CHURCH HURT.

Not only did I grow up as a preacher's kid, but I also grew up as the oldest child and only son of a mega-church pastor in the Detroit area. When I was growing up, the church had over 20,000 members! Not only that, but it was a national ministry with churches all across the country! That had a huge impact on my life, mostly in good ways, but in some bad ways as well.

One of the challenges that I dealt with was how people viewed me. Even when I was just a boy, some people saw me as the heir apparent to my father. Many declared that I was going to be a pastor when I had zero interest in doing so. I had people use me to get close to my father. Some people had a problem with me simply because of who my father was. My sisters had similar and even worse experiences.

Now, don't get me wrong; we went to a great church that was full of great people. However, any time people do life together like they do in a church family (or any other family or group), some simply will not do right. Even those who are good people will have some bad days where they will say and do some things that they wish they could take back. My point is that I experienced church hurt numerous times, probably more than most people.

Beyond that, now I'm a pastor (it turns out that some of those people were right!). The thing about being a pastor is that we experience church hurt, too! Sometimes, people don't realize that church leaders also experience church hurt.

The best example of this may be Jesus. Think about it. One day, Jesus was preaching a message, and the people became so angry that in the middle of His message, they grabbed Him and dragged him out to a cliff, fully intent on killing Him. God delivered Him, but wow—that had to hurt! On another day, Jesus preached a message, and half of His own followers (who had been with Him for a long time) got so angry about their interpretation of what He said that they left Him and never came back. Jesus was brutally betrayed by one of His top twelve guys, Judas. Lastly, the people who were really behind Jesus's crucifixion weren't the Romans but the religious people of His day—the very ones He came to save! Jesus knows church hurt!

Most leaders today don't have to worry about being crucified (although some might be glad to do it to them!). However, they do deal with people mistreating them, gossiping about them, outright lying about them, their church, or ministry, or just leaving their church for nonsensical reasons.

A pain that I've become familiar with is going the extra mile to help someone, only for them to talk about me behind my back. I've had people sit in my own house actively hating me, and I didn't know it at the time—that hurt!

Now, I don't share this so that you will feel sorry for me. I just want you to know that I do know what I'm talking about. I've experienced church hurt, and God has helped me to heal from and overcome it. I believe He's going use me to help you as well.

CHAPTER 2
MY HEALING STORY

As I've shared, as a PK and later a pastor, I've suffered church hurt numerous times. I've been used, manipulated, lied to, lied about, mistreated, berated, betrayed, and more! Praise God, He has healed me from church hurt. However, I do think it will help you for me to dive a little deeper into how He did it. I cannot share many of the details of my story without causing church hurt. However, I believe there are some principles I can share that helped me deal with my lowest moments. It's my prayer that these principles will help you as well.

I've had some really dark moments—I mean really dark. Moments when I not only felt like people failed me, but also that God had failed me (even though He hadn't). I've had moments when I've thought about walking away from ministry. I've had moments when I've thought about no longer living in a way that is right before God. I've had moments where church was the last place I wanted to be. Yet, I still had to go to church, I still had to live right, I still had to minister. I knew in those moments that I simply couldn't stay there. However, it was hard. So, what did I do?

> *And David was greatly distressed; for the people spake of stoning him, because the soul of all the people was grieved, every man for his sons and for his daughter: but David encouraged himself in the LORD his God.*
> —1 Samuel 30:6 (KJV)

My daily prayer life saved me. It saved my family, and it saved my ministry. There were so many days when I entered into prayer, ready to burn everything down. Yet, by the time I had finished thanking God for the good in my life, praising Him for how good He is, worshipping Him for who He is, and spending a significant amount of time (sometimes hours) praying in the Spirit (with some Bethel worship playing on my phone!), I would leave prayer feeling stronger. At least strong enough to get through the day and to the next prayer session the next day. Once I fully discovered this, I found myself going back "to the altar" day after day, month after month, so that God could help me and heal me. And do you know what? He did!

The reward for prayer is joy, and it was His joy that would bubble up in my heart in the darkest of moments that helped me keep my head as God healed my heart.

One of the practices I took on that has changed my life was no longer praying just an hour a day (or so), but praying until I, as the old saints used to say, prayed through. I would pray until I knew my prayer assignment for the day was done. I would pray until I sensed a note of victory in my heart that often would reveal itself in a laugh or a song bubbling up out of me. Some days, that would happen in an hour. Other days, it would be three hours. I learned that in my most difficult, emotional times, I would need to spend additional time with God just to handle things the way that He wanted me to. I also learned the value of something else—patience.

> *That ye be not slothful, but followers of them who through faith and patience inherit the promises.*
> —Hebrews 6:12 (KJV)

God doesn't move in our timing. Sometimes what you would like God to fix in days may take years. That's hard to hear, I know. Yet, I've lived it. God always comes through, God always vindicates, and God always rewards. However, you must learn to cheerfully endure until He does; that's called having patience.

Spending time in God's Word and prayer will help with this. Choosing to trust God's plan over yours will as well. Also, learning contentment is key. You must reach the place where your happiness is not dependent on God fixing your issue, or rests solely in your relationship with God and what He has already done in your life. I've learned to be painstakingly patient. In fact, those around me sometimes complain about it! That patience, though, positioned me to not only heal from church hurt but also allowed God to fully vindicate and restore me. It will for you too!

> *A friend loveth at all times, and a brother is born for adversity.*
> —Proverbs 17:17 (KJV)

Now, don't get me wrong. I did not do this alone. I am not naturally very talkative. I am just fine walking into a social event and having zero conversations. In fact, I'd rather not even walk into a social event at all. It's too draining "peopling"! However, I had to learn to talk a lot to a few people that God had placed in my life to help me deal with church hurt and the other issues I faced. I can't tell you the number of times that I had to pick up the phone and bare my soul to one of those people.

I've found that having God-fearing friends who love and respect you, and who know God's Word, is vital to overcoming church hurt and any other challenges this life brings. In fact, I wore some of those friends out! I have to admit I actually struggle to even reach out to a few of them because I sometimes fear what they think of me now. I've learned that respect is very important to me, and I wonder if they have lost respect for me.

However, even if they have, they got me through! You need to have at least one or two true, godly friends who will not push you away from God and His plan for your life, but toward it, no matter what comes your way.

> *He comforts us in all our troubles so that we can comfort others.*
> —2 Corinthians 1:4

I learned to ask God for comfort. One of the revelations that hit me one day was that God did actually care about how I feel. That's why He offers comfort. He doesn't want me ripped up on the inside trying to serve Him. Sure, there will be times when I have to "play hurt." That is, sometimes you have to continue to play the game for the good of your team even though you are injured. However, He ultimately still wants to bandage you up and make you whole again. Even if it's just to get back out on the field of life and take a few more hits. God will comfort you!

IT'S IMPOSSIBLE TO HEAL WHEN YOU CONTINUE TO THINK AND TALK ABOUT WHAT HAPPENED TO YOU.

I've learned that God truly can heal your heart. I've learned that God can even heal you to the point that being around the very people who hurt you doesn't bother you at all. You can get to the place where you almost forget what happened. God's comfort is that great!

> *And now, dear brothers and sisters, one final thing. Fix your thoughts on what is true, and honorable, and right, and pure, and lovely, and admirable. Think about things that are excellent and worthy of praise.*
> —Philippians 4:8

This might have been the hardest thing for me: to stop thinking about it. I had to learn to stop rehearsing what had happened. I've learned that you can be doing just fine emotionally, but if you start to really think about what someone did to you, it can get you really riled up and hurt you again. I kept doing this! Over and over and over! It was like I was a glutton for punishment. I think part of the reason is that I wanted to continue to vilify the person/people who had done me wrong. What goes along with this is talking about it over and over with others, not for the purpose of getting answers or healing, but simply to vilify them in someone else's eyes as well. Here's the thing: it's impossible to heal when you continue to think and talk about what happened to you. At some point, you have to let it go in your thought life!

One day, God got on me pretty hard about constantly dwelling on and talking about one thing in particular. One of the churches that I previously pastored suffered a church split. I am very justice-minded, and this was a situation that was just wrong! It was very difficult for me to see the impact it had on people that I pastored for nearly a decade, the employees that I had led, as well as the work that I had done to build that church. And I just kept thinking and talking about the injustice of it all until God got on me. He dealt with me to let it go, so I did. I would change the channel mentally when I was tempted to think about it, and censor myself when I was tempted to talk about it.

Ultimately, God healed me of it, and I was able to fully trust that He would make things right in that situation. (The only reason that I am even bringing this up is because I believe God has released me for the purpose of helping you.) Your thought life matters. You must get it under control for you to heal.

> *For God is pleased when, conscious of his will, you patiently endure unjust treatment.*
> —1 Peter 2:19

The last lesson I learned was to do whatever it takes to keep your conscious clear. This means maintaining your integrity, even when others are actively doing you wrong. You see, one day you will stand before God not for what they did to you, but for what you did. You won't be able to blame them for your reaction. God will judge you based on your actions alone. Also, it's when you take the approach that David did with King Saul, when he refused to do any harm to the one who had harmed him, that qualifies you for promotion. When you treat people right, no matter what, God will honor that behavior. God will get you out of trouble. God will promote you into the future that you've longed to have.

Today, church hurt simply isn't the issue that it once was for me. Don't get me wrong, I still have to deal with people doing me wrong. However, it simply doesn't cripple me like it once did. I bounce back easier. I'm much stronger. That didn't happen overnight. God had to help me, and He will help you too!

CHAPTER 3

IS CHURCH HURT A NEW PHENOMENON?

Church hurt is not a recent or exclusively American phenomenon. This is something that happened in Bible days. The Bible tells us, "What is causing the quarrels and fights among you? Don't they come from the evil desires at war within you?" (James 4:1)

Here, James was referencing the fact that the Church, or Christians, were having quarrels and fights amongst themselves. The KJV translation uses the word "wars."

So during this time, Christians were having personal battles with each other. They were even having ongoing wars with each other! So much so that the apostle Paul said in 1 Corinthians 1:11 that he had heard that there were contentions among them. He had heard that they were fighting about numerous things, and his response was to call them really immature. You see something similar in Galatians: "But if you are always biting and devouring one another, watch out! Beware of destroying one another" (Galatians 5:15). This sounds like something that a parent might say to their kids! If you have multiple kids, there are times when they argue and fight with each other.

It was only me and my two sisters in my parents' house. I'm the oldest, and my two sisters were like cats, man! They were always fighting. Of course, I was always innocent; I was never involved. No, but I wasn't as bad as they were. My parents were constantly telling them to chill out! "This is your family," they would say. "Your family members are the very people that you need to have a good relationship with, not fight against." They were right! Thank God my sisters have a great relationship today, and I've got a good relationship with them.

That's what Paul was trying to say in Galatians 5:15. Be careful that you don't bite and devour each other. If a Christian is, in a sense, biting and devouring another Christian, what are they doing? They're hurting them!

They're hurting them through what they're saying and doing! So, we can see here that the early church dealt with church hurt. They had people who were constantly causing and suffering from church hurt. If there were wars and battles amongst them, that means there were injuries and casualties. Now, let's look at what may be one of the first instances of church hurt in the Bible:

> *But as the believers rapidly multiplied, there were rumblings of discontent. The Greek-speaking believers complained about the Hebrew-speaking believers, saying that their widows were being discriminated against in the daily distribution of food.*
> —Acts 6:1

At this point in the Church's history, some exciting things had happened. Jesus had risen from the dead, many people were being healed, and thousands had chosen to believe in Jesus. Christianity was rapidly spreading and had become a huge phenomenon! Of course, Satan, God's enemy, didn't like this. He wanted it to stop. Every time someone believed in Jesus, they left Satan's control and became a threat to him. So, to stop this movement, Satan used the weapon of church hurt! For a while, it worked.

In Bible days, if a woman were a widow, she was almost guaranteed to be poor because her husband was the provider in her home. Also, widows couldn't normally get high-paying jobs like they can today. That meant that these widows needed the support of other people, specifically the church. The church had a daily distribution of food that they provided for the widows. At some point, someone decided the Hebrew widows were more important than the Greek widows, and they distributed the goods based on that belief. They did this for such a long period of time that people began to notice and became upset. The Greek widows were experiencing church hurt. I'm sure they felt like they weren't accepted or valued. This was discrimination, plain and simple! Discrimination in the church was causing church hurt! If you read the rest of the story in Acts 6, you will see that God had a solution for the church that not only fixed the problem but also led to it reaching many more people.

There was another instance of church hurt in the book of Acts, and it was quite personal:

> *Barnabas agreed and wanted to take along John Mark. But Paul disagreed strongly, since John Mark had deserted them in Pamphylia and had not continued with them in their work. Their disagreement was so sharp that they separated. Barnabas took John Mark with him and sailed for Cyprus.*
> —Acts 15:37-39

When Paul and Barnabas embarked on a previous missionary journey, things got a little rough—John Mark just quit. It's kind of like playing basketball against a guy, and when he starts losing badly, he decides to take his ball and go home rather than finish the game. That's what John Mark did. He quit. Now Paul and Barnabas are about to go on another missionary journey, and Barnabas wants to give John Mark a second chance. Paul wasn't having it! The Bible goes on to tell us that the disagreement was so sharp between Paul and Barnabas that they separated.

CHURCH HURT HAS BEEN A PART OF SATAN'S PLAYBOOK SINCE THE BEGINNING.

That's big! When God first started their ministry, one that would become so impactful that it changed the whole world, he had them do it together. They were a tag team. They were God's super-team, and they were now breaking up. All over John Mark!

How do you think he felt about that? How do you think he felt about the great apostle Paul feeling so strongly about him being a failure and a quitter that he actually chose to break up God's super-team because of it? Talk about church hurt! The good news is that Paul eventually came around about John Mark, and God used him to write a book of the Bible called—you guessed it—Mark!

You see, church hurt was a reality in Bible days, too. Satan tried to use it in Jesus's ministry, in the Jerusalem church, and with Paul and Barnabas, and he's still using it today! In fact, church hurt has been a part of Satan's playbook since the beginning. Remember the first murder? In Genesis 4,

Cain and Abel are participating in an offering to God. Abel offers God the best of his possessions, and Cain offers God his leftovers. God accepts Abel's offering, but He rejects Cain's. Instead of learning from this, Cain becomes furious. He doesn't feel accepted. In fact, he is jealous of Abel. He proceeds to murder own his brother over an offering!

So, church hurt is not new. It's been a part of man's existence since the beginning of time.

CHAPTER 4

WHO'S BEHIND CHURCH HURT?

A fun trick that I've played on family and friends at times is to tap them on the shoulder and then run behind someone else who's closer to them than I am. What usually happens is that they look at the person closest to them and think that they are the one who tapped them. Satan, God's enemy, has become a master at this. Why do you say that, you may ask?

The answer is found in Mark chapter 4. In this chapter, Jesus is teaching His disciples about why some people receive God's supernatural results in their lives and others don't. He tells a story about a farmer sowing seed into four different types of ground. The ground is people's hearts, and God's

Word is the seed that will produce God's results. In verse 16, He talks about the second group:

> *These likewise are the ones sown on stony ground who, when they hear the word, immediately receive it with gladness; and they have no root in themselves, and so endure only for a time. Afterward, when tribulation or persecution arises for the word's sake, immediately they stumble.*
> —Mark 4:16-17 (NKJV)

The AMPC (emphasis added) version says that "trouble or persecution arises *on account of the Word*" and that they "immediately are offended (become displeased, indignant, RESENTFUL)."

If a person hears God's words and chooses to believe them, they will have God's supernatural results in their life. However, Satan doesn't want that. When he sees that God's Word has been put in your heart and he knows that it is going to lead to good results in your life, he acts to stop it. You see, he is your enemy just as much as he is God's enemy, and he doesn't want you to have success. He doesn't want you happy. He doesn't want you to go to heaven. He surely doesn't want you telling others about what God did for you and leading them to believe in Jesus as well.

So, as soon as God's Word is deposited in your heart through reading or hearing it (including Bible teaching), he comes to attack you. Those of us who've been around church for a while have experienced the opportunity to apply the preacher's preaching on love before we get out of the parking lot! Do you know what I mean by that? It's like "Why did they just hit my car?" "Why did I just tell them off in the church parking lot!" "Why am I acting crazy all of a sudden?" Well, Satan is behind that. He's trying to get that word out of your heart because if he doesn't, then he's about to lose in some area of your life.

Satan attacks you through tribulation or persecution. That means that bad things happen to you, or people come against you. So much of church hurt is just that, isn't it? People coming against you. Notice the end result of this attack: "immediately they stumble." The KJV translation says they were "offended." I think that's an important word. The AMPC version says they became "displeased and resentful." When these individuals allow offense or anger in their hearts, it stops God's results from happening in their lives.

You may have already experienced this. I know I have. Something bad happens to us, and we are angry at God. We say, "God, why did You let this happen? God, I thought You were good." "God, I thought You said this, or You said that." We become resentful. Here are a couple of questions you need to answer in your heart today:
- Do you resent God right now?
- Do you resent God because of something that has happened in your past or is happening right now?

I want you to notice that the Bible teaches that Satan is behind it! He uses trouble, and he uses people! Satan is the one who causes church hurt, not God. This is so important to understand. Why? Because when bad things happen to us, we tend to take it out on God.

Church hurt is caused by people mistreating you, but we tend to blame God and His institution called the Church, instead of recognizing that this is actually Satan using people to attack us. I like something that a minister friend of mine said: "Church has made many folks upset with God, but God is more than the people at church." Isn't that true? God is more than the people at church. He's much more than them. He is somebody who loves you with an everlasting love. He loves you so much that He sent His only begotten son to come live on this earth and be crucified by His own creation. He loves you so much that He sent Jesus into hell to suffer for three days and three nights in your place. He did all of that so that you could choose between missing hell and going to heaven. The God who did all of that for you is not going to turn around and have fun hurting you.

> *The thief's purpose is to steal and kill and destroy [he comes for their destruction]. My purpose is to give them a rich and satisfying life.*
> —John 10:10 (BBE addition)

That's what God wants. He wants you to have a rich and satisfying life. In fact, if you look at the epistles, which are

Paul's letters in the New Testament, you'll find that God gives many, many instructions to His people about how to treat one another to prevent church hurt, not cause it.

> # GOD DOES NOT HAVE TO USE SATAN'S WEAPONS TO TEACH YOU HIS LESSONS.

One of the fallacies that we have as Christians today—and some preachers preach this—is that God puts you through things to teach you something. Yet, the Bible says in James chapter 1 that when you are dealing with trouble, don't you dare say God did it! God does not send evil to teach you something. Storms don't come to make you stronger. They come to kill you; they come to end you. God does not have to use Satan's weapons to teach you His lessons. He gave you the Bible and placed His Holy Spirit in your heart for that purpose.

That erroneous teaching is one reason why so many end up blaming God for things. "God, why did You do this?" And God says, "It's not Me!" When we are hurt by church people, we look at God and say, "I don't want anything to do with Your Church." That's not fair to God.

Have you ever been blamed or had someone punish you for something that you didn't do? Stinks, doesn't it? It's frustrating. It's infuriating. Yet, if we're not careful, that's what we can find ourselves doing to God. We blame Jesus for people who acted in a way that's completely opposite of how He said to act. When you're dealing with church hurt, that's not God's fault.

One individual said this: "It is really easy to define the church as hurtful when the people inside have wounded you. But the church is not defined by the imperfect people within; it is defined by the head of the church, Jesus." Jesus is not the cause of church hurt in your life—Satan is. Let's stop blaming God for church hurt, and instead, run to Him for the healing that He's made available to us.

The story of Job can easily be misunderstood, just like the issue of church hurt. Job was a really good guy. God really bragged about him. However, he ended up being attacked in some devastating ways. His children died. He lost his wealth. He lost his health. If you're not careful, you'll look at the original KJV translation and say, "Oh, God did that to Job." However, a deeper study will reveal that God didn't do these things to him. In Job chapter 1, we read about the goal of Satan's attack.

> But reach out and take away everything he has, and he will surely curse you to your face!
> —Job 1:11

Satan is telling God that Job only served Him because He had blessed his life. He tells God that if Job were not blessed, he would curse Him. Is that a good description of where you are right now? Maybe when things are going well, you're good with God and with church. Yet, when things get rough, do you find yourself close to cursing God or your church?

If you read the rest of Job, you will find the longest pity party in the history of man! From Job chapter 2 until Job 37, Job has a pity party with some friends. His friends are supposedly trying to help him, but they seem to make things worse. However, one young man really did stand up for God. He makes it clear that Job was wrong. Wrong about what? Job had reached the point of blaming God.

Finally, God got fed up and appeared to Job in a whirlwind. This had to be wild to see. Job is outside, a storm begins, and God talks to him from the middle of the storm. Ever see the movies *Twister*[1] and *Twisters*?[2] Imagine a tornado coming toward you, and it's God. He starts talking to you from the middle of the funnel! That will get your attention! What's worse is that God was not pleased with Job. God addressed Job next from the eye of the storm, and this is what he said:

"I have some more questions for you, and I want straight answers. Do you presume to tell me what I'm doing

---

1 Jan de Bont, *Twister* (May 10, 1996; Burbank, CA: Warner Bros.).
2 Lee Isaac Chung, *Twisters* (July 19, 2024; Universal City, CA: Universal Pictures).

wrong? Are you calling me a sinner so you can be a saint?" (Job 40:6-8, MSG)

God was not happy that Job was blaming Him. He's saying, "Who do you think you are to blame Me?" We have to watch out for this because this is Satan's goal for us, too. That person who criticized you, that person who rejected you, that person who judged you, that person who always wanted to talk about your past, that person who sinned against you—all of those people who attacked you in so many different ways—Satan was using them to push you away from God and His people. Don't give Satan the satisfaction.

CHAPTER 5

GOD CARES

Church hurt hurts. It doesn't just hurt; it's kind of sticky. In a bathroom at my house, I had taped some sticky notes with scriptures to the mirror. They had been there for a couple of years, and one day I decided to peel them off. To my surprise, it took about five minutes to peel off the stickers! That's how church hurt is—it sticks to you. You could find yourself thinking about what happened (and all the negative emotions that come with it) five or ten years later if you don't deal with it correctly. That's why I've written this book: to help you heal from church hurt and to teach you how to properly deal with it so you don't have to continue to deal with it in the future.

In this chapter, let's focus on that healing. Let's start by looking at what God said to Moses about Israel when they were enslaved by Egypt:

> *So the Egyptians worked the people of Israel without mercy. They made their lives bitter, forcing them to mix mortar and make bricks and do all the work in the fields. They were ruthless in all their demands [crushing them under the cruel workload].*
> —Exodus 1:13-14 (MSG addition)

> *Then the LORD told him, "I have certainly seen the oppression of my people in Egypt. I have heard their cries of distress because of their harsh slave drivers. Yes, I am aware of their suffering" [I know all about their pain].*
> —Exodus 3:7 (MSG addition)

The Old Testament is translated from Hebrew, and one word that shows up in the Hebrew to describe what Israel went through is the word "affliction." It means depression and misery. God was saying, "I see what's happening to them. I see how depressed they are. I see how miserable they are. I know their pain." God refers to their prayers to Him as cries of distress. The word cries here means "shrieks of anguish."

This is somewhat similar to how a parent knows their baby's cry of pain. If you are a parent, you know what I'm talking about. You could be at a party with twenty other people. Those people could be talking, playing, and laughing. Your kid could be in the next room. Yet in the middle of all that noise, you recognize your kid's cry immediately, right? That's what God is saying here.

He heard their cry, and He has now appeared to Moses to send him to rescue them.

If you have suffered from church hurt, God has heard your cry, and God has seen what's happened to you. "This was wrong! This hurts. I'm angry. I'm sad!" God has heard it all, and He cares.

Another story that will help us is in Genesis chapter 4. If you know the story of Cain and Abel, you know they really had an issue over church. God had designated a time for them to bring Him an offering. Abel brought the first fruits of the ground. In other words, Abel gave the best of what he had (today we call that the tithe). Cain brought of the fruit of the ground, but not his best. He gave God what was left. So, God accepted what Abel gave Him and did not accept what Cain gave Him. Cain was mad! He was so mad that he ended up murdering his own brother. And in verse 10, God says something very interesting to Cain: "But the LORD said, 'What have you done? Listen! Your brother's blood cries out to me from the ground!'" (Genesis 4:10)

Abel's blood was crying out for justice. He was wronged by his brother, and his blood was expecting God to do something about it.

YOUR GOAL SHOULD BE FOR GOD TO MAKE THINGS RIGHT, NOT PUNISH WHOEVER HURT YOU.

Although the circumstances you're dealing with are different than Abel's, I want you to see once again that God hears your cry! He can hear your heart. He can see the hurt and how you are handling it. He can see the pain that has been caused by someone else's actions. God is a God who will make things right for you. The Bible says in 2 Thessalonians 1:6 that it is right for Him to trouble those who trouble you. Romans 12:19-2 says not to avenge yourself because vengeance belongs to God.

God will take care of what has happened to you or those who have done you wrong. Now, He is also a God who gives people space to repent. In other words, God will allow a person to do something for a while, and judgment doesn't happen right away because He's trying to give that person a chance to get it right. He wants them to recognize that they messed up, come before Him, and maybe even come before you, to ask for forgiveness. We should be okay with that.

I guarantee you that you have messed up sometimes as well, and God has given you space to repent. If God judged us every time we made a mistake, we probably wouldn't be here! Don't expect God to judge people for things they did against you unless you're ready for Him to judge you, too! See, your goal should be for God to make things right, not punish whoever hurt you.

> *"Give all your worries and cares to God, for he cares about you."*
> —1 Peter 5:7

God wants you to give all of your worries to Him. Why? He doesn't want you to worry about anything. Why? He cares about you. Say it out loud, "God cares about me!" He cares about how you feel. He cares if you're heartbroken. He cares if you're confused. Look at how Jesus looks at the people in Matthew chapter 9: "When he looked out over the crowds, his heart broke. So confused and aimless they were, like sheep with no shepherd" (Matthew 9:36, MSG).

There are a number of places in the Bible where it says that Jesus was moved with compassion. His heart hurts, not because of what He's going through, but because of what the people He cares about are going through.

You may have seen commercials that are aired to raise money for needy kids in Africa. They show hungry kids who clearly haven't eaten enough. You can see their suffering, and it makes your heart break. That's how God feels when He looks at people all over the world who don't have Him in their lives. That's why He has people preaching the Good

News about Jesus in churches and has ministries assigned to feed and help people. He cares.

God even cares that someone hurt you at church. The Bible teaches that He knows how many hairs are on your head (Luke 12:7). You don't know the number of hairs on your head, unless you have zero . . . then you know that! Seriously, though, you're that important to Him. The Bible says that as your body was developing in your mother's womb, God paid attention to every detail of its development (Psalm 139).

I remember when my first child was on the way. I had a book called *What to Expect When You're Expecting.* Every month, I could see what was happening with the baby, what stage of development she was at. This is how God was with you! He felt that way about you. The Bible says that His thoughts about you are more than there is sand on the seashore. He thinks about you that much! He cares about you, so He is very aware and bothered by anything that hurts you.

As a father, I've got three daughters. I'm normally a pretty laid-back guy. It takes a lot to get me upset, unless you mess with one of my daughters! I'm still working on that! Even minor things that hurt them can upset me. My kids play sports, and if I feel like a coach is mistreating my kid, I have a hard time. It's like I turn into another person. Why? Because I care about my kids.

God cares about you. When He sees bad things happen to you, He's not looking at you and saying, "Just get over it." He says, "I care about that. I'm sorry that happened to you." First Peter 3:7 tells you to give that care to God because He cares for you so much. God cares about when you've been hurt, and He promises to take great care of you!

CHAPTER 6

LET GOD HEAL YOU

All praise to God, the Father of our Lord Jesus Christ. God is our merciful Father and the source of all comfort. He comforts us in all our troubles so that we can comfort others. When they are troubled, we will be able to give them the same comfort God has given us.
—2 Corinthians 1:3-4

Notice here the Bible tells us that God is a God, not just of power, not just of love, not just of justice, but that He is also a God of comfort. He actually comforts us in all of our troubles. However deep or awful your suffering is, God has made comfort available for you. There is nothing you will go through that is greater than the comfort God has for you. Or, as a lyric of one song goes, "Earth has no sorrow, that Heaven can't heal."[3]

God can make you whole in your heart, no matter what has happened to you. If someone you love has died, if you've been raped or abused, if you've been in the middle of war itself, whatever horrible thing that has happened to you, God can heal your heart.

Jesus said that He had given to Him God's power to heal the brokenhearted. He doesn't just see your heart broken and then pat you on the hand. He has been given Heaven's power to heal it! In Job chapter five, verse 18, the Bible says that God binds up the wounded heart. God is saying to you today that He has a way to heal you on the inside!

WHAT EXCITES GOD IS WHEN HE GETS A CHANCE TO TAKE YOU IN HIS ARMS AND HELP YOU HEAL.

God may have healed you physically, like so many people. Thank God for that! But the same God who heals our bodies heals our emotions. There may be an area of your life right now that has left you broken. You may have tried to sweep

---

[3] The Soul Searchers, vocalists, "Earth Has No Sorrow That Heaven Cannot Heal" by Troy Ramey, December 13, 1992, track # on *Earth Has No Sorrow. . . .*, Atlanta International Record Co., Inc.

it under the rug and ignore it rather than deal with it. You may have decided to just live with it or to act like it didn't happen. However, God doesn't want you to live like that. He wants you healed on the inside. He wants you whole and healthy. That's why He's made his supernatural comfort available to you. He's actually eager to comfort you!

A number of years ago, I hurt my knee playing basketball and ended up tearing something. I went to this doctor I had seen before when I had a more minor issue with it. So, when I visited him this time, he seemed bored. However, when my MRI came back and he could see a tear, he got very excited. He was a different man! He told me that I needed surgery, and he seemed thrilled. I was thinking, "Bro, why are you so excited?!" I realized this is what he cares about: helping people heal. In fact, he cared a little too much because he wanted me to have two surgeries. I only needed one. So, he didn't get to do my surgery!

What excites God is when He gets a chance to take you in His arms and help you heal. He cares; He wants to make you whole again. That's why He's made His supernatural comfort available to you.

So, the question is, how do you take advantage of that supernatural comfort? How do you access it? That's a good question to ask because for God to heal you of church hurt, you will have to work with Him. You have a part to play. The reason why so many of God's children live their lives heartbroken is because they haven't cooperated with God; they haven't let Him heal them.

> *"I tell you, you can pray for anything, and if you believe that you've received it, it will be yours."*
> —Mark 11:24

Notice the word anything here. Clearly, this doesn't just refer to physical or natural things, but also to spiritual things. As we now know, one of the spiritual blessings that God has made available to us is His supernatural comfort. You can be healed on the inside, and He shows us how to get it. When you pray for comfort, believe that you've received it, and it will be yours. You see, when you go to God about anything, you've got to believe you have it when you say, "Amen." You have to believe it before you feel it, before you see it, before anybody else recognizes it. You have to believe that God is so good and so reliable that as soon as you ask Him for comfort, it is done.

When you place an order on Amazon and press the order button, you consider the order done. You then just wait for the delivery. That's how faith works, too. When you make your request of God in Jesus's name, you do so totally persuaded that as soon as you say "Amen," the order is done. The blessing is yours!

When it comes to receiving God's comfort, you need to pray something like this: "Father God, I'm hurting. Please give me supernatural comfort. Heal my Heart, God. I ask it in Jesus's name, and I believe I receive it now. Thank you, Lord; I am now officially comforted!"

When you do that, the order has been placed. You may not feel any different yet, but you believed you received it, so you will.

There's going to be a moment where you realize that God has healed you of that hurt. A moment where it's almost like it never happened. You'll be like those three Hebrew boys who were thrown into the fiery furnace in Daniel chapter 3. When they came out of the furnace, they didn't even smell like smoke! You'll come to a point where, when someone mentions what happened to you, you'll realize that you almost forgot it ever happened!

I got to watch God's supernatural comfort work up close when I was a twenty-one-year-old pastor in Phoenix, Arizona. I'll never forget it because it was the first time that I had to do what some people call a funeral. One Sunday, one of our members was at church like many other Sundays. He was there with his wife and kids. He was in his thirties, and his kids were still pretty young. Sometime that week, he suddenly passed away. His wife was a stay-at-home mother. She didn't have a job, and so not only had she lost the love of her life and the father of her kids, but she had lost her only source of income.

So here I am, twenty-one years old, sitting across from this thirty-something-year-old woman whose life has fallen apart right in front of her eyes. All I knew to do was open the Bible. We started talking about how God would comfort her, how God would give her peace in the middle of this storm. Over time, I watched God do something so supernatural with her. He provided for her every need, and later, she sat in my office and told me about how much the peace and comfort of God had kept her together. I learned then, at twenty-one years old, that this is real. You could be in a really horrible place and completely fine because God is taking care of you.

That's why Paul could write parts of the Bible while he was in prison. In fact, history tells us that his cell was more like a dungeon and that he may have been standing in sewage when he wrote the book of Philippians. He said to "rejoice in the Lord always: and again I say, Rejoice" (Philippians 4:4, KJV). He was writing about joy while standing in sewage! How is that possible? God. God can strengthen you. God can comfort you. God can heal your heart of anything.

The way that you access the supernatural comfort of God is to ask for it, believing that God gives it to you at the moment that you ask Him to. You believe that you've now placed the order and boldly declare that you are not heartbroken anymore. You're not suffering from church hurt. You used to suffer from church hurt, but now you've got God's comfort!

CHAPTER 7
LET IT GO!

God will heal you from church hurt. However, for that healing to last, you need to make another adjustment.

> *"But when you are praying, first forgive anyone you are holding a grudge against, so that your Father in heaven will forgive your sins, too."*
> —Mark 11:25

This scripture is tied to Mark 11:24. Remember that scripture from the last chapter? It tells us how to receive anything that we need from God, including comfort. In other words, if we don't do that part, we'll have a hard time receiving from God. One reason why some people haven't been fully healed on the inside is that they haven't let go of what was done to them. God lets us know here that in the same prayer that you pray for comfort, you must decide to forgive the person who did you wrong.

The word forgive here means to let them go or pardon them. You may be familiar with a governor or a president pardoning an individual of a crime that they have been convicted of. Once pardoned, they are let out of prison. They suffer no longer because of their crime.

UNFORGIVENESS IS LIKE DRINKING POISON AND EXPECTING THE OTHER PERSON TO DIE.

In the same way, we must forgive those who have done us wrong. Let them out of the prison of your heart and mind. Sign the pardon in your heart and let them go!

Notice that Jesus says to forgive anyone whom you hold a grudge against. Anyone. No exceptions.

Sometimes we can read what Jesus is saying here and forgive 90 percent of the people who did us wrong (or forgive them of 90 percent of what they did), but we just don't want to let go of that last 10 percent. However, God said *anyone*. Say it out loud. "Anyone!" Even when someone has done some truly horrible things to you, you need to fully forgive them. Unforgiveness is like drinking poison and expecting the other person to die. It doesn't punish them, but it does hurt you. It prevents you from healing and walking into the future that God still has for you.

I was talking to a friend, and he shared something with me that he heard from a life coach. He said, "All prisoners have a release date. So, when is your spouse's release date?" He mentioned that even a prisoner who's committed a crime and has been judged and sentenced will eventually be let out of prison. When are you going to let your spouse out of prison?

LET IT GO!

Some folks put people in prison forever! We make people serve five consecutive life sentences for what they did to us! God is saying to us today, "That's it. You've been holding on to this grudge, and you need to let it go."

In Matthew 18, Jesus talks about a king who forgave a man of what would be millions of dollars of debt today. That same man then found someone who owed him what was really about $200 and wouldn't forgive him. He had that man thrown in prison! When the king who forgave the man of his multi-million-dollar debt found out, he confronted him. He said, "I forgave you all of your debt, and you couldn't forgive this man of his?" (author paraphrase) He then threw that man into prison.

Jesus was making a point here: God has forgiven you and me of so much more than what anyone has done to us. That's why God requires that you forgive. For you to not forgive is to put yourself in a position where God is not pleased with you. As far as God is concerned, it's only right that you forgive them.

If you've ever been to an outside birthday party with balloons, you know what it's like to see someone release one and let it float away into the sky until you can no longer see it. This is what you may need to do with your grudge right now. You're mad at that pastor, you're mad at the church, you're mad at that man or woman who was supposed to be a Christian.

Beyond church hurt, you're mad at your boss, mad at the White man or Black man, mad at the Democrat or the Republican. Whoever you're mad at today, you need to let it go. Pretend like you have a balloon in your hand right now. Pretend that every grudge you have in your heart is now in that balloon. Now just let go.

Let it go.

Release those people from your prison. Forgive them and release yourself from church hurt. Don't you feel freer? Life is too short to spend it upset at other people.

CHAPTER 8

DON'T PICK THE SCAB

Now that you've let go of that grudge, and God is healing your heart, there is one more thing that I want to warn you about. Beware of picking the scab. Do you know what I mean by that? Have you ever cut yourself and, over time, watched the cut heal? At first, it's an exposed wound, but over time, a scab begins to form where the wound was. Eventually, the cut will disappear, and it will be like the cut never happened . . . unless you pick the scab. If you pick the scab, then you delay that healing. If you do it enough, you can prevent the healing, or, at the least, create a massive and ugly scar. This is what happens when you choose to constantly think about (and talk about) what was done to you.

> *And now, dear brothers and sisters, one final thing. Fix your thoughts on what is true, and honorable, and right, and pure, and lovely, and admirable. Think about things that are excellent and worthy of praise.*
> —Philippians 4:8

Notice what he did not say: "Think about all those times when those church people did you wrong!" That's not in that list, is it? The same thing could apply to a marriage or any relationship in your life. God is telling us to choose not to think about these things. Once you've chosen to let go of what others have done to you, refuse to relive the past. Don't think about it anymore. Don't talk about it anymore. Why? Because when you do, you just peel back the scab. You'll find yourself going to God for comfort again and again because you keep thinking about it and rehearsing it.

You can't change it. If you're like me, you've had this thought: "If I could go back in time, this is what I would tell my younger self. . . ." But you can't; there is no such thing as a time machine. You can't go back. You can't change what you did or what somebody else did to you. So why spend your time thinking about it and getting upset about something that already happened? You've got to learn to change the channel in your mind.

When you're watching television nowadays, it's prudent to have the remote in hand. This is especially true if you have kids. My kids are a little older now, but I remember times when I would just be watching a game with the kids in the room. You would think that would be pretty safe, right? Yet, every once in a while, a commercial would come on that would make me say, "Whoa!" Sometimes it was a movie preview for a horror movie. I knew I had better switch the channel quickly or I was going to have kids sleeping in my bed for days on end!

When a commercial like that comes on, you don't just keep looking at it! You don't just let the kids watch it. You don't say to them, "Check out that spinning head and scary monster, kiddo."

DECIDE TO LET WHAT'S DEAD BE DEAD; DON'T DIE WITH THE DEAD.

In the same way, you can't just keep watching the church hurt channel in your mind. "They did this. This is why they did this. This is why it was wrong. God, I want you to drop lightning from heaven on them right now! Make them a greasy spot!" Every time someone brings up something related to church or church people, like, "I went to this church, and those church people did this, and the pastor did that," I think, *c'mon man! Change the channel! Think about something that is good and just!*

There is a good chance that you have experienced some really great things at church, like many church members. So many of us can say that we've met some great people through whom God has spoken to us. We can tell others that God has healed us or that God has helped us understand our purpose. We can also say that our lives have been changed for the better. When you think about church (or church people), think about the good rather than the bad. That'll help you to heal from the hurt that has been in your heart. Decide to let what's dead be dead; don't die with the dead.

I was listening to a story recently where a minister talked about a climber who climbed a mountain alone. He slipped, and a boulder pinned his arm, and he could not get it out. He tried everything. He chipped away at it for hours on end. After a couple of days, he was running out of food and water. He was going to die. He got to the place where he couldn't even feel his arm. It was dead. So, he had to make a decision. He thought, "Either I'm going to die with this dead arm or I'm gonna cut it off and live." He chose to cut off his arm. He then walked a couple of miles until he found someone to help him, and he lived.

You may be dying with a dead arm. It already happened. There's nothing that you can do about it. You may have allowed it to push you away from God, and now your life is a wreck. You're not enjoying the future that He planned for you. You're getting farther and farther away from Him, and you're dying because you won't cut off what happened in the past. You won't let it go. You've let it keep you from God's people and God's plan for your life. It's time to let the dead be dead. It's time to let the past die and go ahead and live the future that God has for you. It's time to heal.

You'll heal by doing what Jesus did when He was on the cross. He said, "Father, forgive them, for they know not what they do." He dropped any charges in His heart against those crucifying Him in that moment. He didn't think about it anymore. You truly forgive when you choose not to think about it anymore. Then, as you ask God for His comfort, not only will He do it from the inside out, but He will also send people to comfort you. This is one reason why you should stay connected to a church. One of God's purposes for the Church is to encourage each other. The Bible talks about how the tongue of the wise brings health (Proverbs 12:18). God has a way of having people say exactly what you need to hear, when you need to hear it.

I've recently had a couple of conversations like that this week, sitting across from people and looking at them like they're angels, because God has used them to comfort me supernaturally. I thought, "How would you even know to say that? That was exactly what I needed to hear!" That's why you need to stay connected, because although Satan will sometimes use people to hurt you, God will use people to heal you even more. In fact, I trust that He's used this book to do just that.

It's time to heal. Whatever was done to you, whatever happened to you, let it go. Stop thinking about it, stop talking about it. Ask God for His help and comfort, and He will make you whole again. You will be stronger, wiser, and able to do all that He wants you to do in life.

> *"I know what I'm doing. I have it all planned out—plans to take care of you, not abandon you, plans to give you the future you hope for."*
> —Jeremiah 29:11, 13 (MSG)

God said this to His people when they were dealing with a bunch of hurt because of all their mistakes. How much more is this still true for you when others have hurt you? If you'll just stick with God and with His ways, you'll find that your future is bright.

CHAPTER 9

TIME TO GROW

Dear brothers and sisters, when I was with you, I couldn't talk to you as I would to spiritual people. I had to talk as though you belonged to this world or as though you were infants in Christ. I had to feed you with milk, not with solid food, because you weren't ready for anything stronger. And you still aren't ready, for you are still controlled by your sinful nature.
—1 Corinthians 3:1-3

Paul said to the Christians in Corinth that he could only preach to them as though they were spiritual infants. What does that mean? Well, there is a way that you talk to a baby, and there's a way that you talk to a fifteen-year-old. When you're talking to a baby, you might say to them, "Goo-goo, ga-ga." But when you're talking to a fifteen-year-old, you can have a full conversation about the perils of debt. What caused Paul to come to that conclusion? He said that they were being controlled by their sinful nature: "You are jealous of one another and quarrel with each other. Doesn't that prove you are controlled by your sinful nature? Aren't you living like people of the world?" (1 Corinthians 3:3)

What is the sinful nature? The KJV translation calls it "the flesh." Today, we may call it human nature. Human nature left alone is not good. Paul said in Romans 7 three different times that "sin is in our flesh." In other words, if you just do what you always feel like doing, you'll be doing a lot of stuff you shouldn't be doing. That's what was going on with the Christians in this church.

Notice that he said, "Aren't you living like people of the world?" In other words, once you choose to follow Jesus, you should live life on another level. You shouldn't live like everyone else because you are now a part of God's family. You have God in you!

> *You have been believers so long now that you ought to be teaching others. Instead, you need someone to teach you again the basic things about God's word. You are like babies who need milk and cannot eat solid food.*
> —Hebrews 5:12

TIME TO GROW

Imagine if you went to a restaurant in your city, and seated not too far from you was a family. There's a father, a mother, and three kids. The three kids are healthy-looking and appear to be about fifteen, ten, and seven. What would you think if you saw the mother feed baby food to the fifteen-year-old on her lap, as if he was a newborn? You would think something was wrong, right? You might conclude that they have a medical issue because you know that what you are seeing is not normal for a fifteen-year-old.

That's what's happening here in both 1 Corinthians and Hebrews, except that what they were dealing with was a spiritual issue. These individuals just hadn't done what was necessary to grow spiritually. Paul was saying to them that at this point, they should have grown spiritually. They should have grown to the point where he could give them meat instead of baby food. He was disappointed because they were still babes in Christ.

This shows us something important. God expects us to grow spiritually. Just like you can grow mentally, you can grow spiritually. In fact, notice in Ephesians 4 what God is trying to accomplish:

> *Then we will no longer be immature like children. We won't be tossed and blown out by every wind of new teaching. We will not be influenced when people try to trick us with lies so clever, they sound like the truth. Instead, we will speak the truth in love, growing in*

> *every way more and more like Christ [may grow up into him], who is the head of his body, the church.*
> —Ephesians 4:14-15 (KJV addition)

God is making it clear here that He wants us to grow. He wants us to grow to the place where we look like Jesus. He expects us to grow up spiritually.

In Mark 4, Jesus tells us the parable of the Sower. God is the Sower (or farmer), and four types of ground represent four groups of people. Each group responds differently to the words that God plants in their hearts. Notice how the second group responds:

> *And in the same way the ones sown upon stony ground are those who, when they hear the Word, at once receive and accept and welcome it with joy;*
> *And they have no real root in themselves, and so they endure for a little while; then when trouble or persecution arises on account of the Word, they immediately are offended (become displeased, indignant, resentful) and they stumble and fall away.*
> —Mark 4:16-17 (AMPC)

This is the group that hears God's promises and gets excited about them! They are excited about what God has planned for their lives and futures. However, they didn't grow roots, meaning they didn't take the time to ensure that God's words became rooted in their hearts. So, they believe for a little while, but when trouble or persecution shows up, they get upset. The consequence is that God's words don't produce the results in their lives that they or God wanted. It's like God is saying, "I want this in your life. I want you to heal. I want your marriage to be great. I want your career to be amazing. So, I'm giving you my Word to cause those things to happen." However, at the same time, Satan is saying, "I want you sick. I want your marriage broken up. I want you out of work. So, I'm coming to knock that word out of your heart!"

In football, the quarterback hands off the ball to the running back, who then runs down the field, hoping to reach the end zone for a touchdown. However, the other team's defense is also on the field, and they do everything they can to keep the running back from scoring a touchdown. Defenders don't just try to tackle the running back; they try to strip the ball out of his hands. If he arrives in the end zone without a football, his team won't get any points! That's exactly what Satan does. He tries to strip the Word of God out of your heart. What does he use to strip the ball of God's Word from our hearts? He uses trouble and persecution.

Now don't miss this. The difference between this group and the ones who see God's results in their lives is not from a lack of trouble or persecution, but their reaction to it. How does the first group react to the trouble and persecution?

"Then when trouble or persecution arises on account of the Word, they immediately are offended (become displeased, indignant, resentful) and they stumble and fall away" (Mark 4:17, AMPC).

They are offended! That's Satan's goal. What does it mean to be offended? The AMP translation gives us a clue—they become displeased, indignant, and resentful. The word indignant means feeling or showing anger or annoyance at what is perceived as unfair treatment. So, you can be indignant when you get attacked and become angry because you feel like it isn't fair. This shouldn't happen. The word resentful means feeling or expressing bitterness or indignation at having been treated unfairly. What sometimes comes along with being indignant is bitterness.

This is Satan's goal. He wants you to be angry and bitter. He wants you to be upset at people or upset with God. He understands that when you choose to stay offended, the Word that God gave you won't work for you. You might as well have not read those scriptures, heard that message, or prayed that day, because now, the Word won't produce in your life because of your offense. This is a trick of the devil. Remember, he's the one attacking you. He might be using people, but he's the one doing it. He's trying to hinder God's plan for your life. He wants to get you to the point where you're angry. Unfortunately, for so many, this method of attack has worked! We're mad at church people, and we're mad at God, and that's why our lives aren't where we want them to be. God is saying that, at some point, He expects you to stop falling for this trick. He expects you to grow out of it.

> Love (God's love in us) does not insist on its own rights or its own way, for it is not self-seeking; it is not touchy or fretful or resentful; it takes no account of the evil done to it (it pays no attention to a suffered wrong) [Doesn't fly off the handle, doesn't keep score of the sins of others].
> —1 Corinthians 13:5 (AMPC, MSG addition)

Love is not touchy. Love is not resentful. One person said this, "People who aren't easily offended are a breath of fresh air. If you're one of those great people, thank you." Part of the issue for some of us is that we are touchy.

Have you ever been around someone who seems like a ticking time bomb? I played basketball from middle school all the way to college. I never could stand those teammates who seemed to lose their minds over nothing. They just went crazy. They lost their composure. They complained to the referee the whole game. They told their own teammates off. Anytime they didn't get exactly what they wanted, everyone had to hear about it! That's an immature person.

Sometimes, we act this way when we come to church. We complain that someone looked at us in a funny way when they may not have even been looking at us! They were looking past us, but now we're upset. It takes a week for us to get over it, and when we come to church the next week and see them, we're holding a grudge. God is saying, "It's time to grow up!"

IF IT'S EVIL, ADD A D; THAT MEANS IT'S FROM THE DEVIL. IF IT'S GOOD, ELIMINATE AN O; THAT MEANS IT'S FROM GOD.

If you have kids, you know that they believe in all kinds of things when they're young. They may believe in the tooth fairy. They may believe in Santa Claus and more. However, at some point, you expect them to stop believing in those things. In the same way, God expects you to grow up and stop believing this idea that church people are supposed to be perfect.

Grow up!

The Bible doesn't promise us that. It tells us the opposite. God says over and over again that we should put up with each other in love (see Ephesians 4:3). He tells us that even though we may have issues with one another, we should still come together on a regular basis. We need it.

God also expects us to grow past the idea that He is the cause of our problems. God expects us to grow past the thought that it's all His fault. Jesus told us in John 10:10 (KJV) that, "The thief cometh not, but for to steal, and to kill, and to destroy: I am come that they might have life, and that they might have it more abundantly." This is for you and for me. Here's something that may help you: if it's evil, add a D; that means it's from the devil. If it's good, eliminate an O; that means it's from God.

When Satan can get you mad at God, He can't do anything in your life. God is tired of watching you suffer while He stands by with your answer. He needs you to grow up so that He can fix things in your life! God wants you to stop believing Satan's myths and allow Him to make things right for you.

CHAPTER 10

THE CHURCH IS FULL OF HYPOCRITES!

"Do not judge others, and you will not be judge" (Matthew 7:1). A whole lot of people don't seem to know about this scripture! It is interesting that in a time when so many are angry about being judged, we seem to be more judgmental than ever! We judge people in a heartbeat. How many times, just in the last few months, have you seen a story break on social or traditional media that falsely portrays an individual or their actions? When it happens, it's tragic! Partly because people will jump all over the individual in question, calling them all kinds of names or questioning their character. Then, when the actual truth comes out, the damage has already been done.

Jesus says it's better not to judge people; the word judge here is different than what people normally think about. It means to try an individual (similar to putting them on trial) to condemn them, to sentence them. It is also translated as "to decree elsewhere in the Bible."

So, for example, if I say you are a bad person, I'm judging you. Now I'm not judging you if I say you're doing a bad thing. Do you see the difference? Yet, most of the time, when people say, "don't judge me," they are saying that because you said something they did is wrong. Well, they're wrong, because while the Bible does tell us not to judge people, it does also command us to judge behavior.

> *For you will be treated as you treat others. The standard you use in judging is the standard by which you will be judged.*
> *And why worry about a speck in your friend's eye when you have a log in your own? How can you think of saying to your friend, "Let me help you get rid of that speck in your eye," when you can't see past the log in your own eye? Hypocrite! First get rid of the log in your own eye; then you will see well enough to deal with the speck in your friend's eye.*
> —Matthew 7:2-5

> *"Thou art inexcusable, O man, whosoever thou art that judges."*
> —Romans 2:1 (KJV)

These scriptures illustrate how important it is for Christians to mind their own business! We are better off focusing on where we need to grow rather than on being critical of others. We should be removing the logs out of our own eyes rather than the speck in others.

You may be asking, "Pastor Andre, what does that have to do with church hurt?" One of the most prevalent reasons that people don't go to church or have a problem with church is that they're judging church people. "Well, church people are hypocrites." Ever heard that statement? "All preachers are hypocrites!" When a Christian says things like this, they are totally ignoring what Jesus said in Matthew 7.

Not going to church because "everybody is a hypocrite" is like not going to the gym because there are some overweight people there. You stop being a hypocrite by going to church! You're there to let God help you grow, and that's why some people are there!

Declaring that church people are hypocrites and using that belief as an excuse not to go to church is falling for a trick of the enemy, Satan. He actively uses this line of thinking to keep people away from God. You don't get to judge people and then use what they did as an excuse for why you keep doing wrong.

WE COME TO CHURCH FOR HIM, NOT FOR THEM.

I came across a story about a pastor and a lady in his church. The lady said to the pastor:

"Pastor, I won't be going to your church anymore."

The pastor responded, "Why?"

The lady said, "Some members are gossiping about other members. The worship team is living wrong. People are looking at their phones during service. There are so many things wrong in your church."

The pastor replied, "Okay, but before you go, do me a favor. Take a full glass of water and walk around the church three times without spilling a drop on the ground. Afterwards, leave the church if you want."

The lady thought, *too easy.*

She walked three times around the church as the pastor asked. When she finished, she told the pastor she was ready to leave. The pastor said, "Before you leave, I want to ask you one more question. When you were walking around the church, did you see anyone gossiping?"

The lady replied, "No."

The pastor asked, "Did you see any hypocrites?"

The lady said, "No."

He asked, "Did you see anyone looking at their phone?"

"No," she answered.

"Do you know why?"

"No," she replied.

The pastor explained, "You were focused on the glass. You were making sure that you didn't stumble and spill any water."

This is how we are supposed to live our lives! When we keep our eyes on Jesus and grow in Him, we don't have time to see the mistakes of others. You see, we come to church for Him, not for them. Our eyes should be on Him. We go to have an experience with God. God may use people to help you, and He will use you to help others, but it's all about Him. We really need to grow out of using the failings of others as an excuse for skipping out on our time with God.

There are so many prodigals in the world today—people who used to be in church but don't go anymore. Too often, their excuse for living a lifestyle that they know is contrary to what God expects of them is that somebody else isn't living the lifestyle that God expects of them. Whether that person is a pastor, a worship leader, or someone who's been at a church for a long time, you don't get to stand before God in heaven and say that another's behavior is why you did what you did. That won't work for God!

> *Dear brothers and sisters, if another believer is overcome by some sin, you who are godly should gently and humbly help that person back onto the right path. And be careful not to fall into the same temptation yourself.*
> —Galatians 6:1

The MSG translation puts it this way: "If someone falls into sin, forgivingly restore him, saving your critical comments for yourself. *You* might be needing forgiveness before the day's out."

Even if someone in the church does not behave in a way that they should, the Bible teaches that we should humbly restore them rather than talk about them or judge them (James 5:19-20). Part of the problem with the social media mob today is that people are constantly shamed. They face so many critical comments.

I was reading about one particular ministry that was being attacked online, and, to my surprise, I became sad. My response wasn't, "Oh my goodness, look at what they did!"

It was quite the opposite. Why? The Book of Galatians reveals to us that something like that may happen to us if we're not careful. Maturity doesn't mean making critical comments about people online. It doesn't pile on; it prays for and helps restore those people. That's what God expects. He expects us to grow up.

Billy Graham was once asked, "If Christianity is valid, why is there so much evil in the world?" He replied, "Why are there so many dirty people in the world? Christianity is like soap; it must be personally applied if it is to make a difference in people's lives."

CHAPTER 11

THE YELLOW BRICK ROAD

For the Scriptures say, 'You must be holy because I am holy'" (1 Peter 1:16). Some people run from church not because of how people or leaders have treated them, but because they don't want to follow God's standards.

I saw a conversation online where someone was attacking our church. At the time, the church was pretty much brand new. We had just gotten started—like, we had *just* drawn the "F" in Faith Xperience! Well, when I got to the bottom of this person's comments, everything became clear. They were actively living in sexual sin and were upset because the church would not stamp their lifestyle as holy.

I saw a movie years ago. It wasn't the best movie in the world, but I loved it because I like epic movies. It's called *2012*. In the movie, the Earth was falling apart, and this guy and his girl were in a car racing down a road when they saw an old man and a woman on the side. They waved at the man driving the car, trying to get his attention. The man saw them but didn't really understand what they were saying. Suddenly, he saw that the road completely dropped off—it had become a cliff. He barely stopped the car in time. It turns out that the old couple was trying to tell them that the road was out.[4]

The Bible says in Romans 6 verse 23 that "the wages of sin is death." What does that mean? Sin has a paycheck. It doesn't pay up every other week. You might get away with something for a couple of years, but at some point, doing things outside of God's way is going to cost you more than you're willing to pay.

We live in a wicked world that is full of evil and suffering. God has given us Jesus and, through Him, a way to live an impactful and wonderful life. It's like a yellow brick road. If you stay on the yellow brick road, you'll do well. You will have some trouble, but you will overcome it. If you leave the yellow brick road, you get hurt!

Staying on the road is called living holy. Stepping outside of living holy leads to vulnerability to harm and damage that can be life-changing. As churches and Christians, we should

---

4 Roland Emmerich, *2012* (November 13, 2009; Culver City, CA: Columbia and Sony Pictures).

be yelling "road out!" when we see someone heading the wrong direction in life.

If we truly love people, we cannot just stand by and watch them destroy their lives without doing everything we can to save them. Love would not stay silent and let somebody destroy their life.

Sin is fun at first, but eventually it destroys people. Jesus prophesied about the times we are in, a time when sin will abound more and more. The end result is that people will suffer more and more. It is no surprise that our country is suffering more as it embraces certain types of sin more and more. The suicide rate is higher than it's ever been. We've got more mental illness issues. We've got more school shootings . . . and more. Why is all of this happening? Because we keep pushing people farther and farther off God's road and into Satan's arms.

Some people don't want to come to church simply because they just want to keep living the way that they live without anyone telling them that it's wrong. They expect church to be a place where they lift their hands, praise God, hear a message, and then go back home and sin as much as they want. However, a biblical church won't allow that. You can come as you are, but you can't stay the way that you are. We love you too much to just watch you go off the cliff.

If you aren't going to church, you may need to examine your heart. You need to make sure that your issue isn't really with God and His ways, but with church people. The Bible says, "There is a way that seems right to a man, but the end of it is death" (Proverbs 14:12, author paraphrase).

DON'T WANT THAT SIN SO BAD THAT YOU COULDN'T CARE LESS ABOUT GOD OR HIS CHURCH.

The world does what seems right to men, and the end result is a society that has gone off the cliff. The Bible says, "But the way of the Lord is tried" (Psalm 18:30, author paraphrase). God's way is proven, and it produces results in your life.

Choosing to leave God or His Church so that you can freely live in sin is idolatry. The first of the Ten Commandments is, "Thou shall have no other gods before Me" (Exodus 20:3, NKJV). Right? When you chose that sex act, that porn, that man or that woman, that money or that job, that drink or that drug over God, you might as well go ahead and build a statue to it and bow down before it. You've chosen that as your god.

I'm not saying that if you struggle in those areas that you're a horrible person, but what I am saying is that you need to realize that you're struggling in those areas. You need to find out what God says about it and do what it takes to get free of them. You need to get on the yellow brick road of holiness so that you don't fall off the cliff of life. Don't want that sin so bad that you couldn't care less about God or His church.

If you continue on that road, one day you will regret it. When a man has been cheating on his wife and is found out, how does he feel about the woman he cheated with? Often, he wishes that he had never met her. If you were driving drunk and you ended up killing a child, how would you feel? If you're promiscuous sexually and you end up with an incurable STD, how does that make you feel?

See, so many have this mentality that it will never happen to them, but if you decide not to do things God's way, something bad will happen to you. You will one day sit there and say, "I wish I had done this differently." You will realize that you ran from God and church simply because you chose to. You chose to destroy your life.

Give God the opportunity to help you because He can. He's got something better for you than what you're experiencing. There is freedom from every vice and challenge available in God. There is a future where you actually enjoy your life and enjoy making a difference in this world.

Being on God's yellow brick road means doing life with God's people in God's church. It means properly dealing with the fact that sometimes God will use people to minister to you who are themselves flawed. If you read the Bible, you might notice that God mightily used some men and women who had issues! David not only committed adultery, but he also had the woman's husband killed. Moses murdered a man. People argue about Mary Magdalene, but many believed that she was a prostitute when she met Jesus. How about Rahab? She was most assuredly a prostitute. When God's people showed up and she decided to change sides, God honored that. We can go on and on and on. Yet, all these people had a future in God that impacted others.

God is not interested in your past, but He is interested in you not living in sin anymore. He knows that as long as you sin, you can't live the future that He has for you. There's a rap song that I used to listen to, and the lyrics were "I used to do it too. I used to do it too."[5] That's true for so many in the Church. All of us are an ex-something. However, God expects us to eventually be an ex of our sin. He expects us to grow up out of this desire to pick sin over Him.

---

[5] Lecrae, vocalist, "Used To Do It Too" by Lecrae Moore, Brian Taylor, Marlon Montgomery, Kevin Burgess, and Lasann Harris, September 28, 2010, track 6 on *Rehab: Deluxe Edition*, Reach Records.

CHAPTER 12

IS CHURCH REALLY NECESSARY?

As we have discussed in depth, church hurt is real. Some people are hurt through their own mistakes, others because of sin committed against them, and still others because of failed leadership. This reality can leave some reluctant to re-engage with church because they are afraid of being hurt again and want to protect themselves. Some even go as far as questioning whether church has a place in their lives. In this chapter, let's take a look at God's original plan for church and whether He thinks it's really necessary for your life.

> "And let us be moving one another at all times to love and good works."
> —Hebrews 10:24 (BBE)

If you were to go back a few scriptures in this chapter, you would see that Paul is talking about the new life that followers of Jesus now have because of His resurrection and their choice to believe in Him. He repeatedly starts those verses with the phrase, "Let us." He's ultimately stating that there is a right way to live this new life we have in God.

This scripture focuses on how we, as Christians, ought to be moving one another to love and good works. The original Greek words from which this scripture was translated reveal what Paul was getting at: as Christians, we should be coaching one another in taking our next steps in God. We ought to be coaching each other to love God more, to love one another more, to love those who don't necessarily believe in God yet more, and to do good works for God and people.

The next thing that He states is a master key to coaching each other:

"And let us not neglect our meeting together, as some people do, but encourage one another, especially now that the day of his return is drawing near" (Hebrews 10:25).

The BBE translation puts it this way: "Not giving up our meetings, as is the way of some, but keeping one another strong in faith; and all the more because you see the day coming near."

And finally, the MSG says, "Not avoiding worshiping together as some do but spurring each other on, especially as we see the big Day approaching."

The meetings are what we often call church. It's what happens on a Sunday morning. It's what happens in small groups when believers come together to worship and hear from God. Paul is saying that the key to coaching each other is meeting on a regular basis. If you skip meeting with believers, whether in a building, house, or other establishment, then you cannot keep God's instructions to coach one another.

It is hard to coach your brother or your sister if you're not there. I have known and had many basketball coaches, and I can tell you, they wouldn't be good coaches if they rarely or never showed up for practice. They couldn't help their team get better. They couldn't prepare them for their games if they were never there.

That's what Paul is saying. We ought to be coaching each other—helping each other move closer to God and become more like who God wants us to be. However, you can't do that if you're neglecting His instruction to come together. We are supposed to come together so that we can keep one another strong in faith, encourage each other, and help each other experience the future that God wants us to have.

If you're thinking, "I'm okay—I'm fine without church," My question is, "Is okay good enough?" I saw a commercial a while ago that may change how you think about this. There's this guy in the hospital who's about to have surgery. His wife is sitting next to him, and a nurse is standing in front of him. He says to the nurse, "What do you know about the doctor? Is he good?" The nurse says, "Well, he's okay." The man's like ... "okay?" He's visibly getting nervous. Then the doctor walks in and happily exclaims, "Guess who's been reinstated?!" The doctor then asks the guy if he's nervous. The guy says yes, and the doctor responds with: "I'm nervous too. We'll figure it out."

Funny, but not funny, right? Okay isn't good enough, is it? The life that you're living right now is not good enough. You might be surviving. You might make it through the surgery, but you just might not. God is saying, "That's not my plan for you."

Paul was letting them know that this was an issue. Even in that time, there were people who, for whatever reason, thought that you could be a good Christian and yet not consistently be there when believers met together for worship, whether in large groups like Sunday mornings or small groups. If you're thinking the same way, according to the Bible, you are 100 percent wrong.

YOU CAN'T DO LIFE ALONE AND HAVE SUCCESS.

Why? You cannot do everything God wants you to do and get whatever God wants you to have when you're not consistently part of a church family.

Another reason why it is wrong not to regularly go to church is that life is not just about you. I spoke at a men's event recently, and one of the guys asked a question that I think illustrates where some Christians are. He stated that he had a close relationship with God, even though he didn't go to church, so why should he go to church? My answer was because people need you! The church is a hospital as well as a training center. If your relationship with God is that strong, then you can help people who are struggling, and you can help coach people into having their own strong relationship with God. Your relationship with God isn't as strong as you think it is if you're regularly disobeying these scriptures. However, even if I am wrong, your life has a higher purpose than just "doing well."

> *Two people are better off than one, for they can help each other succeed. If one person falls, the other can reach out and help. But someone who falls alone is in real trouble. Likewise, two people lying close together can keep each other warm. But how can one be warm alone? A person standing alone can be attacked and defeated, but two can stand back-to-back and conquer. Three are even better, for a triple-braided cord is not easily broken.*
> —Ecclesiastes 4:9-12

What is God telling us here? You can't do life alone and have success. If you're going to be a successful Christian, you're going to need real, authentic relationships with other people who believe in God. There will be moments when you'll need to be rescued and when you need to rescue others. There will be moments when you will need someone to support you in a tough time. There will be moments when you'll need somebody to protect you from Satan's attacks. If you decide to separate yourself from God's people, you don't get those things. At best, you get an okay life instead of the life that you and God want you to have. You need church, just like your body needs air to breathe. Your spirit needs community. You need it!

In this day and age, a time of great spiritual conflict between God and Satan, it's vital you get connected to a church family. If you don't, you will eventually find yourself going backwards in your relationship with God. You might think that you're doing okay, but you'll find out where you truly are spiritually when things get rough. That's the worst time to find out that you're not as strong spiritually as you need to be.

You know, I love basketball, and, for a while, my daughters did too. I remember one time when my oldest daughter was playing AAU basketball. However, she missed a practice for a friend. She was a good friend and so missed it for a good reason, but she was a little upset about it because she felt like she wasn't going to be as sharp for the next game as she would have been had she gone. I totally understood what she was saying. You can practice all you want on your own, but if you don't practice with the team, you may not be as sharp as you need to be when it's time to play. If you're regularly skipping practice and then you try to show up in a game, you're definitely not going to be ready.

This is how people see their lives get destroyed. It's all a part of Satan's plan. This is how someone shipwrecks their life, leaving you to ask, "How did they end up here? How did this happen to them? How did this happen to their family?" Well, they kept missing out on the times when God had His people come together. You need church.

There are many other analogies for a Christian who is disconnected from a church: a football player without a team, a soldier without a platoon, a tuba player without an orchestra, a lamb without a flock, a child without a family. God does not want His children growing up in isolation, so He created a spiritual family on earth for us. The Christian life is corporate in nature. We belong together. We need each other. You need church.

CHAPTER 13

IS CHURCH ATTENDANCE OPTIONAL?

There is a dangerous belief spreading in our country. It goes like this: "Well, I don't go to church anymore, but I'm still cool with God." Or, you hear others say, "I'm not religious, but I'm spiritual." God doesn't see it that way AT ALL! He sees that you have one foot out the door. You're a step closer to completely leaving Him. You used to have two feet in, and now you have one foot out. You used to come and hang out with Him and His people, and now you refuse to do that. You used to go on dates every week, and now you just want to text every once in a while. Yet you say that your relationship with Him is as strong as it ever was. No, it's not. That is a lie from the pit of hell. That is Satan deceiving you into thinking that you can avoid going to church and still be a true follower of Jesus. The Bible is clear on this issue:

"And let us not neglect our meeting together, as some people do, but encourage one another, especially now that they day of his return is drawing near" (Hebrews 10:24).

"For where two or three gather together as my followers, I am there among them" (Matthew 18:20).

The last place Satan wants you to be is in church. Why? God does great things when His people come together. He does miracles and gives great insight when we gather. When you decide that you no longer need to be among God's people, you miss out on all of that, and that is not what God wants for you.

Another line of thinking is the following: "I know that the Bible says I'm supposed to be a part of a church, but I don't want to do that because the church is hypocritical and judgmental." We've addressed this in another chapter, but let me add this to what we've said:

You are rebelling against God.

The Bible talks about how God gives people something called "space to repent." You may be in that space right now; it's a place where God is merciful to you even though you are doing something that you know He doesn't agree with.

However, you will eventually run out of space, and you'll find yourself doing things you never thought you would do, and your life will be a mess.

God doesn't look at church as an option. As we said, church is not just for you. Other people need you, and He needs you to help them. Some people are far from God and need you to help them find God. When you choose not to be a part of a church community and offer the connection, support, and encouragement that those people need, you're causing God to suffer. You're causing church hurt. Matthew 22 tells us how God sees things: "Jesus replied, 'You must love the LORD your God with all your heart, all your soul, and all your mind'" (Matthew 22:37).

> **GOD DIDN'T ABUSE YOU. GOD DIDN'T SEND THOSE PEOPLE TO YOU. THAT'S NOT A GOD THING. THAT'S A PEOPLE THING.**

God says, "I want all of you." Satan knows this, so he says, "I want to get as much of you away from God as possible." So, he causes some conflict. When you go to church, he causes you to feel shame because of some mistake you made in your past. He works hard to have someone mistreat you, all with the goal of getting you away from God.

CHURCH HURT

Some of us have dealt with awful things at the hands of church people. Those things hurt, but they're not God's fault. We're going to talk about how to properly deal with those things. However, we can't get there as long as you're blaming God. God didn't do those things to you. God didn't use you. God didn't abuse you. God didn't send those people to you. That's not a God thing. That's a people thing.

Sometimes, we unfairly label church as a horrible thing because of what we experienced there. We often have similar things happen to us outside of the church, yet we don't totally bail on whatever "caused" those negative experiences. Nobody ever talks about restaurant hurt. Sure, we've all had bad restaurant experiences. However, that doesn't mean that we never go to a restaurant again. Nobody talks about sports hurt. Any parent who has a child in sports knows that sports hurt makes you want to kill the coach! Yet, we don't force our children to stop playing sports because of it. Sometimes, we talk about relationship hurt, but you know what? Most people dive right into another relationship!

Is church really such an awful place? Or could it be that your issue isn't really with churches? Could it be that you have a problem with God, so you're taking it out on Him by not going to church? If that is the case, you need to know that the farther away you pull from God, the more satisfaction you are giving the one who has actually caused all of the suffering in your life, Satan. You're hurting yourself by walking away from God's plan for your life.

When you say things like, "I don't go to church because of this, that, and the other; I'm better than that," God says, "You're better than Me? You know better than I do?" H says, "I want more for you. I want all of you." You break God's heart when you hold yourself back from God because of what somebody did to you.

> "Come close to God, and God will come close to you."
> —James 4:8

God wants you to constantly come closer to Him. He's waiting for you. You're not coming closer like you should be if you're skipping out on dates with Him and His people. Instead of coming closer, you're getting farther and farther away.

Jesus never skipped church. Have you ever thought about that? Of course, He attended a synagogue, but He didn't stop going to church. If anyone was qualified to skip church, it would be Him, right? He had a great relationship with God on His own. When He went to church, He knew everything the preacher was going to say. He already knew it all.

Every time the preacher made a mistake, He probably thought, "That isn't right. . . ." He went to church with the very people He knew would have Him crucified. He probably sat next to someone and thought, "You're going to be one of them."

Yet, He kept going. Why? His commitment to God. It wasn't about the people and whether they liked Him. It wasn't even about how they treated Him. It was about doing what God wanted. He knew this was a part of God's plan, so He was going to be there. We should follow His example. We've got to recognize that God isn't causing us trouble, so we should stick with God no matter what.

WE'VE GOT TO GET THE IDEA OUT OF OUR HEADS THAT EVERYONE HAS TO TREAT US PERFECTLY FOR US TO GO TO CHURCH.

Joel Osteen once said, "You can be committed to church but not committed to Christ, but you cannot be committed to Christ and not committed to church."[6] Augustine of Hippo allegedly said, "He who does not have the church as his mother does not have God as his father."

Dwight L. Moody said that "church attendance is as vital to a disciple as a transfusion of rich, healthy blood to a sick man." George Barna said:

---

6 Joel Osteen, "You can be committed . . . not committed to church," *BrainyQuote*, https://www.brainyquote.com/quotes/joel_osteen_167166.

> *In the midst of the emotional and spiritual upset that occurs when a church hurts or disappoints us, we tend to lose sight of the fact that the local church is merely a collection of people on a challenging journey, a group of people that are involved in a long-term transformation process.*[7]

See, part of the issue is that we are allowing others instead of God to define church for us. Church is not supposed to be, as one guy said, "A gallery of saints." It's not supposed to be "a display of perfect people." It's quite the opposite. It's a hospital; it's a place where people come to be helped, to grow, and to develop. When you come to a church, you've got to recognize that everybody is an ex-something. I'm an ex-something. I got a couple of some-things I ain't telling you about!

Everyone is in beta testing. Everyone is in development. That means that they might have a bad day, or they might do something that they shouldn't have. We've got to get the idea out of our heads that everyone has to treat us perfectly for us to go to church. You're not at church because of them and you're not at church for them—you're at church for HIM.

I've grown up in church my whole life, yet I'm still a pastor today. How? I didn't let church hurt stop me. I've watched so many of my family and friends who learned the same things

---

[7] Foreword of Stephen Mansfield's *Healing Your Church Hurt: What To Do When You Still Love God But Have Been Wounded by His People* (Carol Stream, IL: Tyndale Momentum, 2012).

that I did, sat in the same services that I did, and went to the same camps that I did, allow their lives to be completely torn apart because of this issue. And it hurts, man. It hurts when I see somebody on social media and look at their life, thinking, *What happened to them?*

For too many, Satan has used this to derail their lives. They have blamed God for what church people have done that destroyed them. Don't let it destroy you. God has an amazing future for you. He didn't say there wouldn't be trouble. He didn't say that people wouldn't bother you. He said the opposite. He said that there will be trouble, that you will be attacked, that people will treat you wrongly, yet He still wants you to love them, pray for them, do good to them, and follow Him so that you can have an amazing future. We need to get back to the psalmist who said in Psalm 122: "I was glad when they said to me, 'Let us go to the house of the LORD'" (v. 1).

Think about it. Has there ever been a time when God spoke to you while you were in church? Has God ever healed your heart in church? Have you ever left church encouraged? Have you ever come to church in pain, and God healed your body? Have you ever been introduced to somebody in church who's become a friend, a brother, a father, or a sister? Have your kids learned some great things in church that have helped them become good kids? I mean, we can go on and on. How many great things have happened to you in church?

Many, many, many, many, many great things have happened to me in church. I've had many unforgettable moments—many faith experiences where God showed up, and my life is better for it. Let's focus on that. Let's get back to the place where we're so hungry for God that we're willing to chase Him into the church, where we praise Him with everybody else, hear what He has to say, let Him heal our hearts, encourage us, strengthen us, and help us to have the future He wants us to have.

I want to challenge you today. Shift your focus. It's not about people; it's about God. It's not about hurt; it's about God's presence. It's not about the past; it's about the future that God has for you.

CHAPTER 14

I DON'T NEED A LEADER

"Remember your leaders who taught you the word of God. Think of all the good that has come from their lives, and follow the example of their faith" (Hebrews 13:7). Paul is talking about leaders. He reveals here that God's plan is for you to have leaders whose example you follow and whose teachings you adhere to.

> Obey your spiritual leaders, and do what they say. Their work is to watch over your souls, and they are accountable to God. Give them reason to do this with joy and not with sorrow. That would certainly not be for your benefit.
> —Hebrews 13:17

In verse 17, he goes a step further: we ought to obey and submit to our spiritual leaders. This is not a popular scripture or teaching! We live in a day and age where we don't want anybody to tell us anything. We say things like "I'm grown. I do what I want when I want." I get it. I've had spiritual leadership say some things to me, and a part of me wanted to bow my back like a cat does before it pounces. I've thought, "Wait a minute, I'm grown! Who do you think you are?" I've had to catch myself because God's way is not my way. My guess is that God's way is not your way, either!

God tells us a few really interesting things here. First, He has made some people to be overseers over your life. There's someone that He is assigned to lead you. That someone is not a businessman. It's a preacher of the gospel. You might be thinking, "But I can't stand preachers!" You're going to have to change your viewpoint! God says, "I actually assigned somebody to you."

Notice that you don't choose this person. You don't get to say, "I like this preacher, so that's the one." In fact, in Acts 20:28, Paul mentions that the Holy Spirit made those preachers overseers. God decides. You don't choose them, nor do they choose you to oversee. It's kind of like your parents. You didn't choose your parents. You weren't in heaven waiting to be sent into the earth swiping right on parents! Some of us might wish we could have done that, but you didn't get to choose, and the same thing is true spiritually. There's somebody that God has called to be your spiritual leader.

If you look at a number of translations, the term "pastoral leaders" is used. This is because the person God has called to lead you is a pastor of a church. God has called you to serve under a particular pastor, which means that God has assigned you to be a part of their church.

You see, you can't "obey them that have the rule over you" if no one has the rule over you. You can't follow spiritual leaders if you don't have spiritual leaders. That's one reason why churches have church membership. Some people say that church membership is not in the Bible. Yes, it is. We may use a different phrase today than "rule over you," but the Bible teaches that when you become a member of a church, you officially show the pastor that they are spiritually responsible for you and that you're going to follow their teaching and example, and even receive their correction.

Here's the kicker. Pastors have flaws. They have issues. Trust me, I'm a pastor. I know I have plenty of issues. I have some things that I struggle with. So, the question is, "Who am I to pastor people?" I've had those moments where I've wanted to say to God, "There has to be someone better for this." Yet if you look at the Bible, you'll find that God uses flawed people. He just does.

God made Solomon the wisest and richest man in the world. Yet, at the end of his life, his heart moved away from God because he lusted for women. He was a flawed man. However, God used him to write the best marriage book ever written, the Song of Solomon. Of course, God used him to write it when he was living right before Him, but the point remains the same. Moses murdered someone. David committed adultery *and* murder!

You will see that God used the people with the most issues to become some of the greatest in the Bible, who impacted the lives of so many. God expected them to grow out of those issues, and most of them did. (God still expects any man or woman of God living today to live right before him, too.) My point is that God is going to call somebody who is flawed in some way to lead you.

Even though your spiritual leader will make some mistakes, God still expects you to follow them. Just because they show a flaw or two doesn't mean that you have an excuse before God to run away from them.

Some people immediately run away from ministers who have fallen—meaning they have done something major they should not have done. They start gossiping about them, they post it on social media, and more. However, just because someone messed up doesn't necessarily mean that God is telling you to leave. Sometimes God will tell you to leave because they have disqualified themselves from overseeing you, but sometimes He doesn't.

God sees and knows things that we don't, and He will direct you on the path that is best for your future. So instead of having a knee-jerk reaction to rumors or even the mistakes of spiritual leaders, pray. Ask God how He would like for you to handle the situation. I've seen situations where God has taken someone who has made some major mistakes and brought them through it into their best season yet. He may want you to be a part of that great season.

We talked earlier about a man in the Bible named John Mark. Remember that he traveled with Paul and Barnabas on their first missionary trip, and when things got rough, he quit. He just went home. So, the next time Paul and Barnabas left for a missionary journey, Paul said that he couldn't come with them. Barnabas disagreed. They ended up having a big argument about it, and they split up over John Mark.

Paul's viewpoint made sense. You can't play games when you're on the mission field; people could lose their lives. You need people with you whom you can fully trust. Today, we might say that John Mark wasn't "ride or die" enough. So, Paul was right, wasn't he? Well, years later, we see Paul publicly recognizing John Mark's value to him in ministry: "Get John Mark and bring him with you to me, because he is helpful to me in my ministry" (2 Timothy 4:11, author paraphrase).

WHERE YOU GO TO CHURCH IS A MATTER OF LIFE AND DEATH!

God ended up using John Mark to write the book of Mark. John Mark had been a quitter, but he clearly finished well. He had a season where he messed up, but God kept working with him, he grew spiritually and became someone who impacted the world.

God will have you follow a flawed leader even as that leader grows. Now don't get me wrong—if a leader has walked away from God or chooses to continue walking in unrepentant sin, he will disqualify himself, and God will deal with him. However, even if God replaced that leader, you wouldn't be released from God's expectation to be under spiritual leadership. He is serious about this issue.

I was at a church in Sacramento preaching for a pastor whom I greatly respect. He and his wife were talking about something that happened in their city that was eye-opening to me. They knew two guys who had contracted the exact same type of cancer at around the same time. One was a part of their church. The other guy attended another church that didn't fully teach the Bible. The guy who was a part of their church survived and was able to live his life. The other guy died. This pastor and his wife said something in unison that I will never forget: "Where you go to church is a matter of life and death!"

You see, when you're under the church or ministry leadership that God wants you in, He can do supernatural things in your life. He sometimes gives you the answers that you've been seeking through your spiritual leaders. You've been praying about it and getting no clarity, but when you get to church, God uses your pastor to give you that answer in his message! Your answer was in your pastor's mouth! Your healing might be in your pastor's mouth. Your wisdom might be in your pastor's mouth. Your financial harvest might be in your pastor's mouth. What you need might be in the mouth of the person God has called to lead you. When you're fully connected to them, you can get what you need, but when you disconnect yourself for any reason, you cut yourself off from the many things that God wants to do in and through your life. It's like being in a shower under the shower head. You can get wet there. However, if you step out from under the shower head, although the water is still running, you will be dry.

Sometimes what we call church hurt isn't really church hurt. Our issue is that we don't like being corrected. We don't want people telling us when we're wrong. However, the Bible teaches that spiritual leaders are supposed to tell those under them when they're missing it. In fact, the Bible says that correction is one of the reasons we have the Bible.

There will be times when you're on the wrong road. In those moments, you need what we spoke about in an earlier chapter—leaders in your life putting up a sign that says, "road out!" Whether you have those leaders in your life and whether you listen to them could be the difference between going off the cliff or making a course correction that leads to good outcomes.

THAT'S THE WAY THIS WORLD IS—YOUR FIRST MISTAKE COULD BE YOUR LAST MISTAKE.

Sometimes, people run from the church when the pastor tells them that they are on the wrong path. Rather than taking the correction that may save them from heartache—or worse—they decide that the church has hurt them.

One day, I ran across a video on social media—a mother deer and a baby deer. The baby deer decides to wander off. A python spots the baby deer, grabs it, and wraps itself around it. Then a lion spots the deer and the python. It fights the python off and eats the deer itself. Poor little deer, right?! All of this happened because the little deer left its mother's side.

This is what happens to Christians all the time. They get a little correction, and they go wandering off. Then the python gets them. They find themselves entangled in sin again or overwhelmed by troubles they cannot fend off on their own. Ultimately, Satan devours them! Sometimes, people find their way home. However, this world is a brutal place, and sometimes the lion gets them. That's the way this world is—your first mistake could be your last mistake. You can't play around.

Doing life with spiritual leaders is one of God's solutions for protecting you from the dangers of this world. As you stay connected to them, they can protect you and guide you on the path that will bring about God's best for your life instead of Satan's worst for it.

> *Is any sick among you? Let him call for the elders of the church; and let them pray over him, anointing him with oil in the name of the Lord:*
> *And the prayer of faith shall save the sick, and the Lord shall raise him up; and if he have committed sins, they shall be forgiven him.*
> —James 5:14-15 (KJV)

You can't call for the elders of your church if you aren't a member of a church. Right? The members of FX church can call my team, and we're there. We counsel them; we show up for a tragedy or a need. However, if we just get a call from a stranger, we can't always show up because we've got to take care of our members. They are my responsibility. They are our responsibility. I'm going to answer to God about how well I took care of them, not someone who hasn't submitted to my leadership. Someone who chooses not to be a member of a church simply will not get all of the benefits of the Christian life that God wants them to have. Also, they are more likely to have to deal with the maximum damage that Satan can inflict on them. You need a church family, and you need spiritual leadership to live the future that God has for you.

CHAPTER 15

IT HAPPENS

"Alright, pastor," you may say. "I hear you. God doesn't want us to skip church. God wants us to be under a pastor, but what about when the pastor or Christians hurt you? Isn't the name of this book *Church Hurt*?" In Ephesians 4, Paul talks about church life. Notice what he says:

"With all gentle and quiet behavior, taking whatever comes, putting up with one another in love; Taking care to keep the harmony of the Spirit in the yoke of peace" (Ephesians 4:2-3, BBE).

The NLT translation says:

> Always be humble and gentle. Be patient with each other, making allowance for each other's faults because of your love. Make every effort to keep

yourselves united in the Spirit, binding yourselves together with peace.
—Ephesians 4:2-3

There will be times when Christians get on your nerves, even your last nerve! There will be times when someone says something they should not have said. There will be times when someone will do something they shouldn't have done. The bottom line is that there will always be an opportunity for church hurt.

Churches are full of people, and people mess up! As one man said, "We're all rough drafts of what we are becoming." I'm still a rough draft. You are still a rough draft. Rough drafts have issues, right? You don't turn in a rough draft because it is not yet complete.

Church is messy. That may be a revelation for you. People tend to think that church is perfect, but it's not. It's perfect when you get to heaven. You won't have to put up with anything when you get to heaven. In heaven, everyone will be happy, loving Jesus and loving on each other. No one will cuss anyone out or gossip about anyone. However, on this earth, church is messy. And it isn't just church—every institution is messy because people are messy.

Sure, should do better at church than anywhere else, and for the most part, we do! Some of the things we complain about in church wouldn't even bother us if they happened in the workplace, because we know that's just how people are, right?

Church is messy, and God knows it. That's why He says that we need to learn to put up with each other in love. What does "in love" mean? It means that we don't cuss each other out because someone cussed us out. We don't get revenge because of what someone did. First Peter 3 does a great job of revealing how we should act at church and toward other Christians:

> *Finally, all of you should be of one mind. Sympathize with each other. Love each other as brothers and sisters. Be tenderhearted, and keep a humble attitude. Don't repay evil for evil. Don't retaliate with insults when people insult you. Instead, pay them back with a blessing. That is what God has called you to do, and he will grant you his blessing. For the Scriptures say,*
> *If you want to enjoy life and see many happy days, keep your tongue from speaking evil and your lips from telling lies.*
> *Turn away from evil and do good.*
> *Search for peace, and work to maintain it.*
> —1 Peter 3:8-11

In Ephesians 4, we read something similar, didn't we? It said to "take care to keep the harmony of the spirit in the bond of peace." God's goal is that even when somebody does you wrong, that you do what it takes for there to be peace.

> *"Do all you can to live in peace with everyone."*
> —Romans 12:18

There's supposed to be harmony among God's people and in church. So, God says that even when somebody does you wrong, make sure that you love and forgive them. He wants you to act like Jesus did to keep that peace in the church. That doesn't mean you shouldn't deal with it—we're going to talk about that in a moment. However, the goal is not to add to the mess. The goal is to try to find a way to work things out so that there is peace. God wants our lives to look a certain way and to have the kind of impact we're supposed to have as Christians and as a church.

GOD BELIEVES YOU ARE BETTER OFF IN A CHURCH WHERE SOMEBODY MIGHT HURT YOU FROM TIME TO TIME THAN OUT OF CHURCH.

God knows that we'll get on each other's nerves at times. Ever been reading an article online and a pop-up window blocks you from reading it? I hate popups. Man, it gets on my nerves. Some websites are so bad that I never go back to them. I just find another way to read the article. That's what happens in life. You'll be living your life, and then there's a pop-up—some person is talking about you at church. Here's another pop-up. Your pastor had a bad day and said something in a way that he probably shouldn't have said it. Maybe they'll come back later and apologize, or maybe they will forget. Here's another example: You're on the way to church and you and your wife get into a fight—a pop-up!

What do you do when a pop-up interrupts your day? Do you click on it, or do you hit the X in the corner and close it out? You hit the X! That's what God tells us to do.

When stuff pops up, you hit the X. You find a way to not give in to the temptation to pop off! You get yourself together and give "the God response." You give the benefit of the doubt. Forgive. Give. Put up with it in love.

This is going to happen, and God tells you how to deal with it. Don't allow the enemy to deceive you into viewing those moments when people do you wrong as an excuse to run away from His people or Him. Instead of running away from them, God says to put up with them in love. Do your part to keep the harmony you're supposed to have. This means that you can do it! It also means that God believes you are better off in a church where somebody might hurt you from time to time than out of church.

God created church so that you could come and be rescued when you need it, could have support when you need it, get God's message when you need it, and experience the presence of God when you need it. He knows that his enemy, Satan, will sometimes slither his way into the church and influence people to say and do things they shouldn't say or do. God is saying to you today not to let Satan accomplish his goal of pushing you away from Him and His people. Don't give Satan the satisfaction of knocking you off the path that God has prepared for your life.

CHAPTER 16
FRIENDLY FIRE

There's a phenomenon among Christians that has gained steam over the last twenty years. It's not that it hasn't always existed in the church, but it seems to have increased at the worst possible time, the time when more and more people are leaving church. I like to call it "friendly fire." Another term that fits well is "church bashing." We seem to be in a time when it is fashionable to bash the church. However, it is not only expected for people far from God to church-bash, but it was prophesied. But this chapter will talk about people in the church—even church leaders—who church-bash.

As I'm writing this, a controversial matter has exploded online against a megachurch and its leader. The controversy is built around how the church chooses to advertise its resurrection weekend services. A leader in the church shared that they don't use the words resurrection or the blood of Jesus in their advertisements so that people far from God will be more likely to attend their church and hear about Jesus. Mind you, this leader made sure to explain that their church believes and teaches about the blood of Jesus, the resurrection, etc., and I can confirm that is true, having been familiar with this ministry and its pastor for many years. They believe and teach all the basic and vital tenets of Christianity. However, many Christians have seen it fitting to attack this church. There have been articles written about it, reels and TikToks posted, and emails shared and more about their Easter flyers!

However you feel about their soul-winning strategy, isn't it just a bit ridiculous to make so much out of a church's marketing strategy? We're not talking about their doctrine or some scandalous behavior, but their flyers and ads! By the way, this happens to be a church that has literally impacted millions for Jesus, not only through their church services in person and online, but their music. Even if you don't 100 percent agree with some of their doctrine, it's clear that they are preaching Jesus and filling heaven.

This is just one example of an issue in the church that, let's be honest, comes from Satan himself. Not so sure about that? Check out this scripture:

> *But Jesus knew their thoughts, and said to them: "Every kingdom divided against itself is brought to*

> *desolation, and every city or house divided against itself will not stand."*
> —Mathew 12:25 (NKJV)

We've said before that the one person who doesn't want people to go to church is Satan. Let's add to that: he is also the one person who wants the church divided. Why? Because a church divided is less effective in heaven's war against him. That means more people suffer and go to hell. Awful, right? Yet, we are in danger of experiencing that when we constantly attack other Christians, ministries, and ministers. Also, we are clearly violating scriptures like the one below:

> *Who are you to judge another's servant? To his own master he stands or falls. Indeed, he will be made to stand, for God is able to make him stand.*
>
> *But why do you judge your brother? Or why do you show contempt for your brother? For we shall all stand before the judgment seat of Christ.*
>
> *Therefore, let us not judge one another anymore.*
> —Romans 14:4, 10, 13 (NKJV)

One fallacy that is very prevalent in the church today is the idea that the Christian's job is to "correct" the wrong doctrine of other Christians or ministries. If I had $100 for every time I read a comment online calling a well-known minister a heretic or their teaching heresy, I'd be one of the richest men in the world!

MANY TAKE ON THE RESPONSIBILITY OF THE APOSTLE PAUL WHEN THEY ARE THE APOSTLE OF NONE!

Something is wrong with this approach. First, all too often, it lacks humility. Many times, people who call Christian leaders heretics or their doctrine heresy are totally wrong in their criticism. They've taken a clip that they've seen online out of context, they are misinformed about what someone is actually teaching, or they simply don't know the Bible as well as they think they do. Beyond that, it actually isn't our place to correct everyone, even those we think may be off. I could hear someone saying, "But that is what Paul did! Shouldn't we do what Paul did?" Let's look at some examples and see what we can get from it:

> *I can hardly believe the report about the sexual immorality going on among you—something that even pagans don't do. I am told that a man in your church is living in sin with his stepmother. You are so proud of yourselves, but you should be in mourning and sorrow and shame. And you should remove this man from your fellowship.*

Even though I am not with you in person, I am with you in the Spirit. And as though I were there, I have already passed judgment on this man.
—1 Corinthians 5:1-3

Cling to your faith in Christ, and keep your conscience clear. For some people have deliberately violated their consciences; as a result, their faith has been shipwrecked. Hymenaeus and Alexander are two examples. I threw them out and handed them to Satan so they might learn not to blaspheme God.
—1 Timothy 1:20

Do you notice a pattern here? Paul primarily addressed those under his spiritual leadership. What you don't read about is Paul correcting those under James, Peter, or John's leadership. He also addressed serious matters of sexual sin and people abandoning their faith (not the content of their church flyers). Even when he addressed the Galatians' false teachings, he did so because what they had received turned them away from the "gospel of grace" and back to a gospel of works.

If you are not the spiritual leader over those you publicly correct and rebuke, then what are you doing? One reason why correction is reserved for spiritual leaders is that they have been called, anointed, and trained, and they have the experience necessary to judge rightly. So many take on the responsibility of the apostle Paul when they are the apostle of none! It is best to leave public correction to the ministry's spiritual leadership and God. Simply put, it's not your job!

In my city, a police officer from Wixom cannot arrest someone committing a crime in Detroit. Why? The police officer is out of their jurisdiction. Only Detroit police officers could arrest those committing a crime in Detroit. Well, if you are busy policing other ministers or ministries besides those under your spiritual authority, you are out of your jurisdiction!

Far too often, what we call correcting others is actually nothing but slander or gossip. If there is any group that you don't want to be guilty of slandering, it's God's ministers.

> *"Do not touch My anointed ones, And do My prophets no harm."*
> —1 Chronicles 16:22 (NKJV)

> *Then he went up from there to Bethel; and as he was going up the road, some youths came from the city and mocked him, and said to him, "Go up, you baldhead! Go up, you baldhead!"*
> *So he turned around and looked at them, and pronounced a curse on them in the name of the LORD. And two female bears came out of the woods and mauled forty-two of the youths.*
> —2 Kings 2:23-24 (NKJV)

> *Now as the ark of the LORD came into the City of David, Michal, Saul's daughter, looked through a window and saw King David leaping and whirling before the LORD; and she despised him in her heart.*
>
> *Then David returned to bless his household. And Michal the daughter of Saul came out to meet David, and said, "How glorious was the king of Israel today, uncovering himself today in the eyes of the maids of his servants, as one of the base fellows shamelessly uncovers himself!" So David said to Michal, "It was before the LORD, who chose me instead of your father and all his house, to appoint me ruler over the people of the LORD, over Israel. Therefore I will play music before the LORD.*
>
> *Therefore Michal the daughter of Saul had no children to the day of her death.*
> —2 Samuel 6:16, 20-21, 23 (NKJV)

We ought to be very careful about criticizing God's ministries and ministers. As you can see in the scriptures above, God simply doesn't take it lightly. We need to have enough reverence before God to keep our mouths off of His men and women. Your slandering of God's ministers and ministries may be one of the reasons why God can't further bless what you're doing in your life and ministry. You may very well be fighting against God Himself!

> *And now I say to you, keep away from these men and let them alone; for if this plan or this work is of men, it will come to nothing; but if it is of God, you cannot overthrow it—lest you even be found to fight against God.*
>
> *And they agreed with him.*
> —Acts 5:38-40 (NKJV)

If even the Sanhedrin council, the very council that sentenced Jesus to crucifixion, saw the wisdom in this, shouldn't we? Even if ministry leaders have truly fallen, we should be doing what the Bible says in Galatians 6:

> *Dear brothers and sisters, if another believer is overcome by some sin, you who are godly should gently and humbly help that person back onto the right path. And be careful not to fall into the same temptation yourself.*
>
> *Pay careful attention to your own work, for then you will get the satisfaction of a job well done, and you won't need to compare yourself to anyone else.*
> —Galatians 6:1, 4

The keyword here is humility. You see, you don't have it all right; neither do I. You believe some doctrine, behave a certain way, or use some method that is wrong. When we get to heaven, God will correct us all in some way. Have the humility to recognize this: we're all growing. If someone believes in Jesus, preaches Jesus, and wins people to Jesus, that's my brother and my sister, even if we don't fully agree on everything. As a church leader, you will have to do what Paul did at times: address teaching that is not consistent with scripture. You will have to show people what the Bible actually says, and when you do, do it with humility.

I was at a minister's conference when one of my spiritual leaders, Kenneth Copeland, did this. I was so impressed with how he addressed some doctrine that was a little off in the church. He didn't attack the ministers who were teaching it; he lovingly gave them the benefit of the doubt while teaching what the Bible actually says on the topic.

Kenneth Hagin once talked about a time when God corrected him mid-sentence while preaching a message. At the time, he was a Baptist minister who didn't believe in speaking in tongues. He found himself criticizing "tongue talkers" in one of his messages, and the Holy Spirit convicted him. He said that he stopped his message and apologized to his people.

He told them that he had no business saying what he said and that he really didn't know anything about speaking in tongues. Of course, later on, he learned about speaking in tongues and began to do so himself. He then spent decades helping millions to speak in tongues as well.

Teach your people what the Bible says when there is error in the church, but also be an example to them in how you handle it—with humility and care. Too often, there's fire coming out of the pulpit, but it is not the fire of God aimed at burning up the works of the devil; it is fire aimed at other ministers.

Let's be honest, jealousy plays a role in some of this. There's this feeling that "I have been as or more faithful to God as that minister, and I am not having the kind of impact that they have." Thus, we are all too eager to poke holes in who they are or what they are doing, and if they happen to make a mistake, look out! They'll really get it now! That's what the Bible calls "the flesh." It is of the flesh, even when ministers do it. Remember that it was the priests of the day who so forcibly orchestrated the crucifixion of Jesus! Why? Out of jealousy!

We need to stop. We need to grow up. We need to rejoice with our brothers and sisters when God uses and blesses them mightily. We are on the same team. We need to help restore them when they miss it.

> *"Nor give place to the devil."*
> —Ephesians 4:27 (NKJV)

Satan wants the church divided. He wants to see Christians writing books and articles, typing comments, making reels and TikToks, and sharing emails that attack other Christians. He's using all of that to continue to steal, to kill, and to destroy people throughout this earth. Let's stop giving him what he wants. Instead, let's give Jesus what He wants.

> "May they experience such perfect unity that the world will know that you sent me and that you love them as much as you love me."
> —John 17:23

This is what Jesus wants from us. This is what the world needs from us: a unified church, a church that loves God and loves each other. A church that knows how to deal with disagreement and failure correctly. There's enough "church hate" going around in the secular world. We simply shouldn't participate in that.

> Above all, you must live as citizens of heaven, conducting yourselves in a manner worthy of the Good News about Christ. Then, whether I come and see you again or only hear about you, I will know that you are standing together with one spirit and one purpose, fighting together for the faith, which is the Good News.
> —Philippians 1:27

Let's be the church by being for the church. Let's unite as the church in pushing back the gates of hell in this earth and help as many as possible go to heaven!

CHAPTER 17

CHURCH ISN'T WACK

How many miracles happened to people at church in the Bible?

One Sabbath day as Jesus was teaching in a synagogue, he saw a woman who had been crippled by an evil spirit. She had been bent double for eighteen years and was unable to stand up straight. When Jesus saw her, he called her over and said, "Dear woman, you are healed of your sickness!" Then he touched her, and instantly she could stand straight. How she praised God!
— Luke 13:10-16

This woman was healed at what we call a church service today!

> *While they were at Lystra, Paul and Barnabas came upon a man with crippled feet. He had been that way from birth, so he had never walked. He was sitting and listening as Paul preached. Looking straight at him, Paul realized he had faith to be healed. So Paul called to him in a loud voice, "Stand up!" And the man jumped to his feet and started walking.*
> —Acts 14:8-10

This man was healed at a church service!

> *Jesus went into the synagogue again and noticed a man with a deformed hand. Since it was the Sabbath, Jesus' enemies watched him closely. If he healed the man's hand, they planned to accuse him of working on the Sabbath.*
>
> *Jesus said to the man with the deformed hand, "Come and stand in front of everyone."*
>
> *Then he said to the man, "Hold out your hand." So the man held out his hand, and it was restored!*
> —Mark 3:1-3, 5

This man, like many during Jesus's ministry, was healed at what we would call a church service today! Even in the Old Testament, there were numerous times where God's people came together and God's presence just rolled into the room and did miraculous things.

> "For where two or three are gathered together in My name, I am there in the midst of them."
> —Matthew 18:20 (NKJV)

Most people who have been in church could easily think of times when they experienced God doing supernatural things for them and others, whether in a church, a large group setting, or a small group setting. We have experienced miracle after miracle after miracle. We recently had an evangelist minister healing to many in one of our church services. We saw results right there on the spot, and people's lives were changed forever. I've been in services like that my entire life, and there's nothing like it!

The miracles that so many have experienced and the blessings that we've received from church are so much greater than whatever hurt we've had. Sometimes we've come to church and felt like we were about to jump off a cliff but got just what we needed to go on another day. Sometimes, we needed some encouragement and received it. Sometimes we needed answers from heaven and God gave them to us. Sometimes, we needed our faith strengthened or our bodies healed, and God did it. Many have believed God to find the love of their life and found them while serving at their church. God does so many great things at church that many books could be easily filled with people's stories. There are far more people who are happy with their church and pastor than there are who are staying out of church because of church hurt. God does so much for us through our church family, and we need to stay connected even when church hurt pops up to harm us. Church isn't wack. It's awesome.

Just like anything else in life, church comes with an instruction manual. If you read and follow the instructions, then you will get out of church what you should. If you don't, then church life may not be the blessing it's supposed to be in your life. So, in this chapter, I want to give you some rules for church life.

GIVE YOUR LIFE TO IT

"They committed themselves to the teaching of the apostles, the life together, the common meal, and the prayers" (Acts 2:42, MSG).

"Every day they were in the Temple and homes, teaching and preaching Christ Jesus, not letting up for a minute" (Acts 5:42, MSG).

God is showing us here that you have to sell out to church. I like what Craig Groeschel said that when you are planted, the church is not a destination. It's an identity and who you are.[8] Church is part of your identity and that should be true the rest of your life.

---

8 Craig Groeschel, "Stop Going to Church with Pastor Craig Groeschel," Filmed 6 Aug. 2018 at Life.Church, Sunday sermon, 36:58, *YouTube*, https://www.youtube.com/watch?v=zXDYzzxUi9s.

BELIEVE THE BEST OF PEOPLE

"Love bears up under anything and everything that comes, is ever ready to believe the best of every person" (1 Corinthians 13:7, AMPC).

We have learned that we are to put up with people in love. Here we see that love is ever ready to believe the best of every person. What does that mean? When someone has done you wrong, love doesn't assume that they did it for awful or evil reasons. Love assumes that they didn't really mean it the way you took it; they must've had a bad day, even though it may not even be true. Love gives people the benefit of the doubt. As Stephen M.R. Covey said, "We often judge ourselves by our intentions and others by their behavior."[9] If we choose to believe the best of people, we will learn to look at other's people's intentions as well.

DON'T BE TOUCHY

> *It is not conceited (arrogant and inflated with pride); it is not rude (unmannerly) and does not act unbecomingly. Love (God's love in us) does not insist on its own rights or its own way, for it is not self-seeking; it is not touchy or fretful or resentful; it takes no account of the evil done to it [it pays no attention to a suffered wrong].*
> —1 Corinthians 13:5 (AMPC)

---

9 Stephen M.R. Covey, *The Speed of Trust: The One Thing That Changes Everything* (New York, NY: Free Press, 2006).

Do you know someone who can't stand to be touched? They almost lose it if you sit next to them and accidentally touch them! Let's be honest, that's a bit weird! I don't know how someone like that makes it through life. You can't be that way in church life, either. I'm not talking about being touched physically. I'm talking about being touched emotionally. As we can see in these scriptures, love is not touchy. In other words, it doesn't become irritated or angry quickly. It doesn't get upset quickly.

> *"Hannah was praying in her heart, and her lips were moving but her voice was not heard. Eli thought she was drunk."*
> —1 Samuel 1:13 (NIV)

Hannah was a barren woman who believed God for a son. She sat in church and prayed to God from her heart, but didn't say words. The preacher walked up to her and said, "Did you come to church drunk?" She easily could have been offended. She could have gone off on him. I think many would have! However, she wasn't touchy. She explained that she was just praying to God. Soon enough, God gave her what she was praying for, a son named Samuel. I'm not so sure that she would have had her miracle baby if she had decided to be touchy at church.

A woman came to Jesus for Him to heal her daughter. Notice what Jesus says! "It isn't right to take food from the children and throw it to the dogs" (Matthew 15:26).

He called her a dog! Now, of course, He was making a spiritual point. Yet, instead of rolling her neck, snapping her fingers, and posting about it, or worse, her response was amazing.

> She replied, "That's true, Lord, but even dogs are allowed to eat the scraps that fall beneath their masters' table."
> "Dear woman," Jesus said to her, "your faith is great. Your request is granted." And her daughter was instantly healed.
> —Matthew 15:27-28

You can't afford to be touchy. At some point, you've got to grow up beyond reacting so quickly to slights. Some people almost look for someone to do something wrong to them. They walk into church life expecting the worst and are ready to give the worst.

WHEN PEOPLE START MESSING WITH YOU, JUST STRETCH YOUR WINGS OUT AND GO HIGHER.

There's a bird called a crow. Crows are pesky and like to mess with eagles. Eagles are majestic. Watching them fly can be breathtaking. However, sometimes crows come behind eagles and accost them. Eagles are so big that it's hard for them to turn. Crows, on the other hand, can turn quickly, so they like to pick on the eagles. When they do, eagles just stretch out their wings and fly higher and higher. They fly to heights where the crow can no longer breathe, and the crow gets dizzy and faints. You've got to learn to be an eagle. When people start messing with you, just stretch your wings out and go higher. Ignore it. Just keep living the life God has for you.

FORGIVE QUICKLY AND EASILY

> *Get rid of all bitterness, rage, anger, harsh words, and slander, as well as all types of evil behavior. Instead, be kind to each other, tenderhearted [vs. hard-hearted], forgiving one another, just as God through Christ has forgiven you.*
> —Ephesians 4:31-32 (author addition)

"Then Peter came to him and asked, 'Lord, how often should I forgive someone who sins against me? Seven times?' 'No, not seven times,' Jesus replied, 'but seventy times seven!'" (Matthew 18:21-22)

When Jesus said "seven times seventy," He didn't mean to count to 490! He didn't mean that you are free to have your own "purge," like the movie, as soon as you get to 491! He means that we should forgive people every single time, no matter what they do to us. That doesn't mean there aren't consequences for their actions. However, it does mean that you should choose not to carry a grudge in your heart against them. Forgive them even if they don't ask for it.

SPEAK UP WHEN YOU'VE BEEN WRONGED

> *If another believer sins against you, go privately and point out the offense. If the other person listens and confesses it, you have won that person back. But if you are unsuccessful, take one or two others with you and go back again, so that everything you say may be confirmed by two or three witnesses. If the person still refuses to listen, take your case to the church. Then if he or she won't accept the church's decision, treat that person as a pagan or a corrupt tax collector.*
> —Matthew 18:15-17

> *So if you are presenting a sacrifice at the altar in the Temple and you suddenly remember that someone has something against you, leave your sacrifice there at the altar. Go and be reconciled to that person. Then come and offer your sacrifice to God.*
> —Matthew 5:23-24

God does not like unresolved issues between His people. Part of the reason we have church hurt is because we've never actually addressed the events that caused it. Sometimes, people are mad at you, or you're mad at people, and one party doesn't even know that they hurt the other party.

I had a couple of incidents like this in my life, one where I did something wrong and one where I didn't.

A few years back, one of the young men that I pastored in a previous church reached out to me through Facebook. He was a young guy when I pastored him, so young that I had done his premarital counseling. I didn't even know he was upset with me. He told me that he had been upset with me for a number of years because when his father died, I really didn't step up like he needed me to. That hurt.

I quickly realized what happened. I had injured my knee playing basketball and had just had surgery. I literally could not walk. I was stuck sitting at home with something sticking in my knee. So, when his father passed, I asked my ministers to go to his house to minister to him and his family. I let the ministers handle the entire bereavement process. Having said that, he was right. I should have done more. I allowed my recovery to distract me, and I had to apologize to him.

I had another guy who was upset with me reach out about a situation where I actually did everything that I could to help him, and he simply would not listen to me. After he did his own thing, things did not work out, and he, at least partially, blamed me. He was wrong.

The point is, at least both came to me, and that's God's system. God doesn't want you walking around holding something against somebody. You should approach them and let them know what's going on. Just do it the right way because you can say the right thing the wrong way and create even more damage.

Be sure not to cause church hurt for someone else by gossiping or sowing discord. Handle your situation in a way that would make God happy, like discussing it with spiritual leaders, if necessary.

Here is the other side of this: it is very likely that at some point, you will be the cause of someone else's church hurt. You may not mean to, but at some point, someone may point to you and say that you did them wrong. When that happens, be sure to do what the Bible says in James 1: "Wherefore, my beloved brethren, let every man be swift to hear, slow to speak, slow to wrath" (James 1:19, KJV).

You need to be humble enough to hear what they have to say. You need to be mature enough not to immediately get angry or defensive. You need to be quick to admit when you are wrong and apologize so that there can be peace.

RESTORE THOSE WHO HAVE MESSED UP
"Live creatively, friends. If someone falls into sin, forgivingly restore him, saving your critical comments for yourself. *You might be needing forgiveness before the day's out*" (Galatians 6:1, MSG).

When someone in the church makes a big mistake, we ought to restore them. We should save our critical comments for ourselves because we might need forgiveness ourselves pretty soon. Don't talk about them, criticize them, or be awful to them. Let's check out this story.

A man went to church, and he forgot to switch off his phone. It rang during prayer. The pastor scolded him, the worshipers admonished him for interrupting the silence, and his wife lectured him about his carelessness all the way home. You could see the shame, embarrassment, and humiliation on his face, and, after all this, he decided to never step foot in a church again. That evening, he went to a bar. He was still nervous and trembling. He spilled his drink on the table by accident. The waiter apologized and gave him a napkin to clean himself. The janitor mopped the floor. The female manager offered him a complimentary drink. She also gave him a huge hug and a peck, saying, "Don't worry, man, who doesn't make mistakes?" He has not stopped going to that bar ever since.

THE NUMBER ONE PURPOSE OF CHURCH IS TO REACH PEOPLE WHO ARE FAR FROM GOD.

Sometimes our attitude as believers drives souls to hell. You can make a difference by how you treat people, especially when they make mistakes.

REMEMBER, IT'S NOT ABOUT YOU

> *If a man has a hundred sheep and one of them gets lost, what will he do? Won't he leave the ninety-nine others in the wilderness and go to search for the one that is lost until he finds it?*
>
> *In the same way, there is more joy in heaven over one lost sinner who repents and returns to God than over ninety-nine others who are righteous and haven't strayed away!*
> —Luke 15:4, 7

> *Are they servants of Christ? I know I sound like a madman, but I have served him far more! I have worked harder, been put in prison more often, been whipped times without number, and faced death again and again. Five different times the Jewish leaders gave me thirty-nine lashes. Three times I was beaten with rods. Once I was stoned. Three times I was shipwrecked. Once I spent a whole night and a day adrift at sea. I have traveled on many long journeys. I have faced danger from rivers and from robbers. I have faced danger from my own people, the Jews, as well as from the Gentiles. I have faced danger in the cities, in the deserts, and on the seas. And I have faced*

> *danger from men who claim to be believers but are not. I have worked hard and long, enduring many sleepless nights. I have been hungry and thirsty and have often gone without food. I have shivered in the cold, without enough clothing to keep me warm.*
>
> *Then, besides this, I have the daily burden of my concerns for all the churches.*
>
> —2 Corinthians 11:23-28

When it's all said and done, you are going to heaven if you're actively following Jesus. How many people in the world around you are not? How many of those people need you to connect with a platoon, a church family, so that together you can reach them?

The number one purpose of church is to reach people who are far from God. Church exists to reach that woman who was caught in adultery, to deliver the guy who's possessed by demons, to help the Mary Magdalenes of the world. We, as a church, not the pastor or an organization, but as a people, are here to reach those who are from God and help them experience the future that God has for them.

As long as hell is a real place, our priority can't just be our comfort or our feelings. Our priority has to be reaching them. At some point, we have to grow up to the point where we stand back up again and do everything God has told us to do, even if we are beaten, whipped, and stoned like Paul. We recognize that we have family members, friends, and colleagues who are going to hell and that we need the church to work with us in doing everything we can to help them go to heaven. Not only do you need church, but others need you in church so that God can use you to save their lives forever.

CHAPTER 18

FOR PASTORS ONLY

Church hurt is a very real issue for pastors. In fact, an argument can be made that pastors deal with church hurt feel the hurt more than anyone. I know. As I've shared, I have been in ministry for almost thirty years. I have been an assistant youth pastor, a campus ministry pastor, a young adult pastor, a co-pastor, and a lead pastor.

The majority of my time in ministry has been spent in the lead pastor role. I started out co-pastoring a church in Phoenix, Arizona, when I was twenty-one years old. Then I transitioned to pastoring what became a borderline mega-church in Atlanta for almost ten years. Following that experience, I pastored a mega-church in Southfield, Michigan, for four years before I settled into my current role as lead pastor of Faith Xperience Church. What's my point? I have been hurt by church people over and over again. I also grew up in a pastor's home and have seen my parents hurt by church people in ways that even I have yet (and hope to never) to experience.

What does church hurt look like for a pastor? Let me count the ways! Earlier, I mentioned a more recent experience I had. I knew someone in my church who was struggling to make ends meet. I felt led to hire this person who seemed to have a skill set that could help the church, but helping was the main reason I felt God wanted me to hire that person.

At first, this arrangement seemed to work out well. However, over time, the person grew distant. I reached out a number of times, offered to help with some personal issues, and more. Eventually, that person decided it was time to leave the employ of the church. I had no problem with that. I know God often has us in different roles in different seasons.

However, I later found out that the person had violated my trust by sharing sensitive information from a confidential meeting and led a group of people who were actively speaking against me (and my church), not only in personal conversations but also online. That hurt. Unfortunately, as pastors, we know from experience that too often the ones we help the most are the ones who will stab us in the back.

I could tell you many other stories—*many* other stories. In fact, I posted this question online: "What causes you as a pastor or minister to feel church hurt?" Here are a few of the responses:

- Gossip, slander, undermining, unhealthy expectations, and lack of support.
- When people you've invested significant time, energy, effort, and money into suddenly ghost you without a word.
- When those who once believed in you and supported you quickly create factions against you because of their own offenses (betrayal by those who are supposed to be in the foxhole with you).
- People having an issue with you but talking to everyone but you about it.
- When other pastors or ministers openly speak against you, and you find out from someone else.

Church hurt as a pastor can be the result of:

- People mistreating your kids because they are your kids.
- People mistreating your spouse because they are your spouse.
- People misrepresenting something that you said in the pulpit.
- People spreading false rumors about you.
- People "telling you off."
- People verbally attacking you or your church online.
- People leaving your church for insignificant reasons.
- People stealing from you or the church.
- Other pastors splitting your church.
- Other pastors or ministers attacking you publicly.

There are so many more reasons!

Notice what's consistent across this list: people—the very people that God has called us to serve—cause all of it! This creates a bit of a dilemma. How can God expect you to serve the people when it's the people who are hurting you? How can God expect you to give your life to the church when the church hurts you?

> *Now get to your feet! For I have appeared to you to appoint you as my servant and witness. Tell people that you have seen me, and tell them what I will show you in the future. And I will rescue you from both your own people and the Gentiles. Yes, I am sending you to the Gentiles to open their eyes, so they may turn from darkness to light and from the power of Satan to God. Then they will receive forgiveness for their sins and be given a place among God's people, who are set apart by faith in me.*
> —Acts 26:16-18

Paul understood this. When God first spoke to him about his calling, He told him that He would deliver him from the people and yet send him to the people, particularly the Gentiles. Throughout his ministry, Paul found himself dealing with intense persecution from people whom he had preached to. Some even followed him from town to town, trying to hinder his message. It went so far that this happened:

"And there came thither certain Jews from Antioch and Iconium, who persuaded the people, and, having stoned Paul, drew him out of the city, supposing he had been dead" (Acts 14:19, KJV).

ULTIMATELY, WE SERVE IN MINISTRY FOR GOD, NOT FOR PEOPLE.

Talk about church hurt! Paul was doing what God called him to do, and the very people that he was trying to save stoned him! This happened in Acts 16 as well:

> *A mob quickly formed against Paul and Silas, and the city officials ordered them stripped and beaten with wooden rods. They were severely beaten, and then they were thrown into prison. The jailer was ordered to make sure they didn't escape. So the jailer put them into the inner dungeon and clamped their feet in the stocks.*
> —Acts 16:22-24

This didn't just happen to Paul. Remember what happened to Jesus?

> When they heard this, the people in the synagogue were furious. Jumping up, they mobbed him and forced him to the edge of the hill on which the town was built. They intended to push him over the cliff, but he passed right through the crowd and went on his way.
> —Luke 4:28-30

The people interrupted Jesus's message, not for a song or a "tongue and interpretation", but to kill Him! Some people didn't like your message. . . . but have they tried to kill you because of it? Wow!

Let's just say it—church hurt is an occupational hazard when you're serving the church! Yet, God has called us to serve the church and the community. He expects us to. In fact, one day He's going to hold us accountable for whether we did it faithfully.

You might be thinking right now, "How am I supposed to serve when I feel like this, when I hurt like this, when I know that more is to come?" Here are some answers.

REMEMBER WHO AND WHY YOU SERVE

> And so, dear brothers and sisters, I plead with you to give your bodies to God because of all he has done for you. Let them be a living and holy sacrifice—the

> kind he will find acceptable. This is truly the way to worship him.
> —Romans 12:1

There are a number of reasons why we serve God, but this has to be near the top of the list: we serve Him because of all that He has done for us. Jesus came, was tortured and murdered, went to hell, and then rose again for us. Not only that, but He has protected us, provided for us, comforted us, and been so merciful to us! Just take a few minutes and think about the details of all that God has done for you. It's overwhelming, isn't it? We could never pay God back, but we can give back to Him by helping as many people as possible become a part of His family.

> "For we speak as messengers approved by God to be entrusted with the Good News. Our purpose is to please God, not people. He alone examines the motives of our hearts."
> —1 Thessalonians 2:4

Ultimately, we serve in ministry for God, not for people. We want to please Him, not them. We want to bless Him by blessing them. This is our motivating factor, and it needs to drive us no matter what comes our way.

> *"Then Jesus explained: 'My nourishment comes from doing the will of God, who sent me, and from finishing his work.'"*
> —John 4:34

We care about what God cares about because we love Him. We know that He cares about people knowing Him, finding freedom, discovering their purpose, and making a difference in this world. Therefore, we have dedicated our lives to that cause, too. That is why we are in the ministry. Don't forget it!

KEEP THE PROPER PERSPECTIVE

"Love bears up under anything and everything that comes, is ever ready to believe the best of every person" (1 Corinthians 13:7, AMPC).

Although there are surely some in your church or ministry who have caused (or will cause) you to experience church hurt, it's important to remember that they are the minority. It's not everyone. It's not even most of them. For every Judas, there's a John, James, Stephen, Timothy, or Titus.

Most of the people that you serve absolutely love you and will be a blessing to you. Even the Peters of the bunch, who may have seasons where they don't always say and do the right thing concerning you, will find a place of repentance and grow.

This is why it's better to approach people the way Paul said to in 1 Corinthians 13: "believe the best of them." See and treat everyone as innocent until proven guilty! Don't buy the enemy's lie that church is your problem because it really isn't; it's just some people in the church. The church itself (and church people in general) is one of the greatest blessings of your life!

FORGIVE, FORGIVE, FORGIVE

"Jesus said, 'Father, forgive them, for they don't know what they are doing.' And the soldiers gambled for his clothes by throwing dice" (Luke 23:34).

There aren't many more profound ways to be like Jesus than to forgive someone who has wronged you. This is especially true when they don't recognize, acknowledge, or ask for forgiveness for what they have done wrong. True leaders forgive.

> *"Most important of all, continue to show deep love for each other, for love covers a multitude of sins."*
> —1 Peter 4:8

Remember that to forgive is to truly let go of what they have done to you, to pardon them. From time to time, our government officials will pardon someone for a crime that they committed. That pardon doesn't always say that they didn't commit the crime, but that they no longer have to pay the price for it. That's a place that we need to get to with those who have hurt us. Some people have been in the prison of our minds and hearts for a long time, and it's time to let them go!

By the way, forgiveness doesn't just help them—it helps you! At some point, you have to stop rehearsing what someone did to you in your mind and in conversations and move forward. Sometimes it's that very act of forgiveness that can actually lead to healing for you. It can also lead to reconciliation with those who have done you wrong.

DON'T BARK BACK

"He was oppressed, and he was afflicted, yet he opened not his mouth: he is brought as a lamb to the slaughter, and as a sheep before her shearers is dumb, so he openeth not his mouth" (Isaiah 53:7, KJV).

The leading priests, the teachers of religious law, and the elders also mocked Jesus:

> *"He saved others," they scoffed, "but he can't save himself! So he is the King of Israel, is he? Let him come down from the cross right now, and we will believe in him! He trusted God, so let God rescue him now if he wants him! For he said, 'I am the Son of God.'" Even the revolutionaries who were crucified with him ridiculed him in the same way.*
> —Matthew 27:42-44

As a leader, you must learn to ignore personal attacks. Notice how, even when Jesus was on the cross, He didn't bark back at those who mocked Him, though He really could have! I don't know about you, but if I were in His position, I would have been tempted to mock them back with all the details of how they would burn in hell! However, Jesus didn't do that.

Kenneth Hagin is one man of God who had the greatest impact on my life as a young minister. He often came under attack (still does!) because of the message of faith that God had him share. Many people have lied about him and misrepresented his message. There were times when his spiritual sons became a bit frustrated with him because they wanted him to respond to his critics, but he refused. As a younger man, I didn't always understand this, but I do now.

I once heard a statement that stuck with me: "No one pays attention when a dog barks at the moon, but everyone does when the moon barks back!" You have to remember that you are the moon in that story. It's beneath you to respond to the attacks of those whom Satan is clearly using. God will vindicate you. You simply focus on letting Him use you.

TAKE IT; DON'T GIVE IT

> *Greatly desiring to see thee, being mindful of thy tears, that I may be filled with joy;*
> *Be not thou therefore ashamed of the testimony of our Lord, nor of me his prisoner: but be thou*

> *partaker of the afflictions of the gospel according to the power of God.*
> —2 Timothy 1:4, 8 (KJV)

Timothy had been through it! He was hurting and, at the very least, was tempted to draw back from his assignment because of it. God had Paul write this letter to him so that he would continue to "stir up the gift in him" and "be a partaker" of the trouble that sometimes comes with preaching the gospel. Notice what Paul didn't say. He didn't say that Timothy wouldn't face more trouble. He didn't say that he wouldn't be hurt again. He said, "step up and take it." He went on to talk about enduring hardship as a good soldier of Jesus in the next chapter.

As we said, church hurt is an occupational hazard when you're serving the church. Yet, God still expects you to serve the church! At some point, you have to develop thick skin and be willing to take whatever hits come your way for the sake of the gospel message. When football players step onto the field at the beginning of the season, they do so knowing that there is a 100 percent injury rate in football. They do it anyway because they love football and the rewards that it brings them. We ought to love God and love people enough to step on the field of ministry and stay there. We also ought to be tough enough to take the attacks of people without attacking back.

> *For this is commendable, if because of conscience toward God one endures grief, suffering wrongfully. For what credit is it if, when you are beaten for your faults, you take it patiently? But when you do good and suffer, if you take it patiently, this is commendable before God.*
> —1 Peter 2:19-20 (NKJV)

> *"Not returning evil for evil or reviling for reviling, but on the contrary blessing, knowing that you were called to this, that you may inherit a blessing"*
> —1 Peter 3:9 (NKJV)

It is vitally important that you maintain a clear conscience toward God, including when people attack you. Once again, God will avenge you. God will vindicate you. If you maintain a clear conscience even in tough times, God will still be able to use you mightily.

BELIEVE GOD FOR COMFORT

> *All praise to God, the Father of our Lord Jesus Christ. God is our merciful Father and the source of all comfort. He comforts us in all our troubles so that we can comfort others. When they are troubled, we will be able to give them the same comfort God has given us.*
> —2 Corinthians 1:3-4

Now, don't get me wrong. God does not want you to go through life hurting. It's especially difficult to minister well with a broken heart. So, what do you do when you're hurt, even as a minister? The same thing you do as any believer. Ask and believe God for His supernatural comfort. God can fully and totally heal your heart until there isn't even a scar! You may be wiser because of what you experienced, but you won't be bitter. You can be a pastor who is whole and happy while serving God and His people. You just have to let God heal you from time to time.

REMEMBER THE REWARD
"His lord said to him, 'Well *done*, good and faithful servant; you were faithful over a few things, I will make you ruler over many things. Enter into the joy of your lord'" (Matthew 25:21, NKJV).

One of the things that keeps us going in life is knowing that if we do well, there will be a reward. As a kid, I remember being promised a gift if I did well in school, and that motivated me. As an adult, it motivates me to work out consistently if I know that I will like what I look like in the mirror. My wife's response to romance motivates me to be romantic, too!

God understands this. He created us this way! And there's no greater reward than to hear Him say, "Well done." However, there is one pretty close reward, and that is hearing him say it to those we have helped come to Jesus.

> *"For what is our hope, or joy, or crown of rejoicing? Is it not even you in the presence of our Lord Jesus Christ at His coming?"*
> —1 Thessalonians 2:19 (NKJV)

One of the reasons that Satan causes church hurt is to distract us. Don't let him. Keep your eyes on the prize! You are pleasing God and helping others do the same. You will be marvelously rewarded for it, not only in this life, but more importantly, in the one to come!

CHAPTER 19

CHURCH HURT AND PREACHERS' KIDS

Growing up as a preacher's kid (PK), I have not only been around my family's ministry my entire life, but I have also been around many other PKs. I've also been around individuals who may not be the biological sons of spiritual leaders but are their spiritual sons or daughters. One thing I have learned is that many people in these positions also fight the same battle against church hurt. Unfortunately, too many lose that battle. If you are a PK or a spiritual son or daughter, I don't want that for you.

In the next three chapters, we're going to dive into the topic of church hurt in ministerial families, natural and spiritual. This one may be a little touchy to tackle, but I believe it's going to lead to some healing!

There are three main types of church hurt that PKs and spiritual sons deal with. The first is church hurt from dealing with the people that your parent(s) serve, such as members of their church. The second is from your parents or other family members who are in the ministry. And a third type is from individuals verbally attacking your parents. In the next few chapters, I will focus primarily on the first two.

Collateral damage is a term that many in our country understand and is defined as "any incidental and undesired death, injury or other damage inflicted, especially on civilians, as the result of an activity. Originally coined to describe military operations, it is now also used in non-military contexts to refer to negative unintended consequences of an action."[10] Very often, PKs are collateral damage. Although the church is a family, there are often many internal battles going on among its people, as Paul said in 1 Corinthians 3 and Galatians 5:

"For you are still carnal. For where *there are* envy, strife, and divisions among you, are you not carnal and behaving like *mere* men?" (1 Corinthians 3:3, NKJV)

"But if you bite and devour one another, beware lest you be consumed by one another!" (Galatians 5:15, NKJV)

---

10 Wikipedia, "Collateral damage," *Wikipedia*, 5 March 2025, https://en.wikipedia.org/wiki/Collateral_damage?utm_source=chatgpt.com#cite_note-Holland2007-1.

Also, James mentions the same: "What is causing the quarrels and fights among you? Don't they come from the evil desires at war within you?" (James 4:1)

All too often, individuals who are still carnal (as Paul called them) attempt to harm other believers, including their spiritual leaders, in particular.

When they cannot get to those leaders directly, they will attack their children. Those attacks are often verbal. Sometimes, they are subtle; other times, they are passive-aggressive. However they come, as PKs, we know how it is!

One of the things about being a PK is that you really get to know people. I don't know many groups of people who can read people better than PKs! Unfortunately, we gained that knowledge through the school of hard knocks. We've had people be mean to us, lie about us, and even find ways to punish us (for example, a Sunday School teacher) because they are angry at our parents. I recently did a podcast with my sisters where we dove into this issue. We told a few stories, but boy, do we have a bunch more! If you're a PK, I'm sure you have or have heard some stories, too!

PKs also deal with people attempting to get close to them so that they can be close to their parents. We've had friends who tried to spend the night at our house just so their parents could see where we live and check out our house.

I remember an employee who worked for my dad who would play basketball with me at the church. He seemed really nice to me, and I really took to him. One day, our relationship suddenly changed. I later suspected that I was just a tool that he was using to ingratiate himself with my father.

This is just a glimpse of the world that PKs live in. Is it the worst thing in the world? Not at all. I remember sitting at dinner with a pastor of a large church in Paris, France. We were talking about these issues, and he mentioned that growing up as a PK is a lot better than growing up as the child of a drug addict or criminal. He's right!

However, one challenge of being a PK is facing the dangerous phenomenon in the lives of developing young boys and girls—church hurt. We can quickly recognize how different our lives are from everyone else's, how different our challenges are, and that those challenges are often the result of church people or our church life. If we don't deal with church hurt correctly, it can derail our lives.

Yet, some of us are still struggling with church hurt, even as adults! So, what do we do about it? I think Paul's instructions in two places in scripture are especially applicable to us.

> *Get rid of all bitterness, rage, anger, harsh words, and slander, as well as all types of evil behavior. Instead,*

> *be kind to each other, tenderhearted, forgiving one another, just as God through Christ has forgiven you.*
> —Ephesians 4:31-32

We have to make the heartfelt decision to let it all go! We have to let go of the bitterness, let go of the anger, and let go of the harsh words that were spoken to us. Instead, we must forgive. Just as God has forgiven us of all that we've done wrong, we need to truly forgive every single person who caused us church hurt. Only then will we find healing.

Also, we must remember to separate God from His people. They are not the same. Do not allow what church people did to you to separate you from God or the purpose that He has for your life. Frankly, that is what Satan is after. He hates PKs! He wants to push them as far from God as possible so that he can ruin their lives.

PKs ARE KNOWN FOR RUNNING FROM CHURCH, AND ALTHOUGH IT'S OFTEN BECAUSE OF CHURCH PEOPLE, TOO MUCH OF THE TIME, IT'S BECAUSE OF THEIR PARENTS.

Additionally, what better tool than a wayward PK to drive others far from God? He can deceive others into thinking that if following Jesus didn't work for the PK, it surely wouldn't work for them. Lastly, Satan understands something that many of us understand as well. Most PKs are called into the ministry themselves. He will do everything in his power to stop them from taking up their parents' mantle and being used by God to have an even greater impact for God than they did. This is why, if you're a PK called to ministry, you must get free from people. Free from what they say, think, or do to you. Only then can you God fully use you to help them.

> *"Delivering you from the people and from the Gentiles, unto whom now I send thee."*
> —Acts 26:17 (KJV)

It's vitally important to live your life for an audience of One—Jesus—as Peter did: "Obviously, I'm not trying to win the approval of people, but of God. If pleasing people were my goal, I would not be Christ's servant" (Galatians 1:10).

An even greater challenge for PKs is when a relationship (or lack thereof) with their parents) causes church hurt. PKs are known for running from church, and although it's often because of church people, too much of the time, it's because of their parents. For some of us, the issue is that our parents simply don't prioritize use over their ministry. God's order in the home is God first, spouse second, children third, then ministry work. However, some of our parents didn't get the memo! We ended up with a part-time parent(s) who put ministry concerns and events ahead of our own challenges and games. Instead of being at your game, your father was at a church meeting. Instead of holding you when you dealt with the heartbreak of your first breakup, your mother was busy holding a church member's hand due to a fight they had with their spouse. When we needed them, they were not there because of the church!

If this is you, it's clear why you feel the way that you do. Unquestionably, you were robbed of God's best for you. A minister's first ministry is in the home, and somehow your parent(s) missed that. What now? Here's a blueprint:

1) **Consider a conversation with your parents.** "If another believer sins against you, go privately and point out the offense. If the other person listens and confesses it, you have won that person back" (Matthew 18:15). Pray about it, and God will not only tell you when the time is right for a conversation but also the right words to say.

2) **Choose to forgive them, even if you think they don't deserve it.** Someone once said that walking in unforgiveness is like drinking poison, hoping that someone else will be harmed. Unforgiveness will rob you of the future that God has for you. At some point, you need to fully let go of what they did or didn't do and how you feel about it.

> *"Love . . . is ever ready to believe the best of every person."*
> —1 Corinthians 13:7 (AMPC)

Giving them the benefit of the doubt will also help. Most PK parents don't even realize the mistake they have made in this area. They had no intention of not being there for you. Even though that is not an excuse, it does matter.

3) **Ask God to make things right for you.** "Father to the fatherless, defender of widows—this is God, whose dwelling is holy" (Psalm 68:5). God has a way of filling the gaps in our lives. He is a God who can send people our way who will be a great blessing to you. He is a God who can take what Satan meant for evil and turn it for our good. As we've discussed in this book, He is also a God who can totally and completely heal your heart.

4) **Do better when it's your turn.** "Fathers, do not provoke your children to anger by the way you treat them. Rather, bring them up with the discipline and instruction that comes from the Lord" (Ephesians 6:4). Sometimes what you learn from a parent or mentor is what not to do. As a PK who has lived through this, you know how it feels. Make sure that you don't repeat the mistakes of your parent(s). Parents, make your children a priority over the ministry (or any career). That will help heal you as well.

I have a friend of mine who lost his father to a car accident when he was young. I watched firsthand how not having a father in his life impacted him. However, I also watched God eventually bless him with five sons, to whom he is a great father. That's the kind of God we serve. Stick with Him. Don't give the enemy what he wants.

The thing about being a PK is that you know God. You know His voice, you know His tug on your heart, and you know He has a great plan for your life. Don't let this challenge stop you from being all that God made you to be!

CHAPTER 20

CHURCH HURT AND FAMILY MINISTRY

God calls families. Throughout the Bible, we see family members sharing callings and anointings—from Aaron and the Levites to the line of kings that ruled Israel. The same is true today. Many times, as they grow into adults, PKs discover that God has called them into the ministry just like their parents. Many times, they are called to serve in ministry *beside* their parents (at least for a season of their lives). This is a great blessing for both the parents and the PK. The parents get to serve with their children, which is not only enjoyable as a parent but also beneficial to the ministry in multiple ways. PKs get the benefit of having built-in mentors who also love them! They receive personalized training, ministry opportunities, and, often, the privilege of carrying on the legacy their parents have forged.

However, families doing ministry together can come with significant challenges. If not done correctly, it can divide families, destroy marriages, derail callings, and damage ministries. As a PK who has lived in the ministry world my entire life, I've seen all of it. You may be nodding your head right now as you are reading this because of your own experiences. At times, it seems like family and ministry just don't mix!

If you've been hurt by family in ministry, the same solutions apply to you as we have discussed before. Although sometimes the greatest hurt and harm can come from those we're closest to and trust the most, we must make the heartfelt decision to forgive them. Remember this story?

> *Then Peter came to Him and said, "Lord, how often shall my brother sin against me, and I forgive him? Up to seven times?"*
>
> *Jesus said to him, "I do not say to you, up to seven times, but up to seventy times seven. Therefore the kingdom of heaven is like a certain king who wanted to settle accounts with his servants. And when he had begun to settle accounts, one was brought to him who owed him ten thousand talents. But as he was not able to pay, his master commanded that he be sold, with his wife and children and all that he had, and that payment be made. The servant therefore fell down before him, saying, 'Master, have patience with me, and I will pay you all.' Then the master of that*

servant was moved with compassion, released him, and forgave him the debt.

But that servant went out and found one of his fellow servants who owed him a hundred denarii; and he laid hands on him and took him by the throat, saying, "Pay me what you owe!" So his fellow servant fell down at his feet and begged him, saying, "Have patience with me, and I will pay you all." And he would not, but went and threw him into prison till he should pay the debt. So when his fellow servants saw what had been done, they were very grieved, and came and told their master all that had been done. Then his master, after he had called him, said to him, "You wicked servant! I forgave you all that debt because you begged me. Should you not also have had compassion on your fellow servant, just as I had pity on you?" And his master was angry, and delivered him to the torturers until he should pay all that was due to him.

So My heavenly Father also will do to you if each of you, from his heart, does not forgive his brother his trespasses.
—Matthew 18:21-35 (NKJV)

No matter what someone has said or done to you, whatever awful outcomes you may be dealing with because of the behavior or actions of others, you must forgive. You also must stay on assignment, even if it's difficult right now. You don't get to quit just because things are tough!

> *Servants, be submissive to your masters with all fear, not only to the good and gentle, but also to the harsh. For this is commendable, if because of conscience toward God one endures grief, suffering wrongfully. For what credit is it if, when you are beaten for your faults, you take it patiently? But when you do good and suffer, if you take it patiently, this is commendable before God.*
> —1 Peter 2:18-20 (NKJV)

Ouch! Not my favorite scriptures at all, yet this is scripture. There are times when you have to take mistreatment, even from family, to maintain a clear conscience before God. First Corinthians 13:4 (NKJV) reveals that, "Love suffers long *and* is kind"!

We've talked about other scriptures that address how to handle situations where someone does you wrong. For example, we know to respectfully address issues with someone who has wronged us. That's a healthy practice. We are to do that even if it may not be well received (their reaction is their responsibility). Sweeping issues under the rug is not healthy for any relationship. Also, Scripture has revealed that it is God who will avenge you should it come to that.

WHEN IN BAD SITUATIONS, SEEK GOD ABOUT HIS VICTORY PLAN FOR YOUR SITUATION AND FOLLOW IT.

You see, your responsibility is to find a way to keep a clear conscience in light of whatever is going on. It is absolutely appropriate to enforce biblical boundaries in your relationships. However, no matter what, never ever dishonor your parents, as the scripture says, 'Honor your father and mother,' which is the first commandment with promise" (Ephesians 6:2, NKJV). If we're not careful, we'll read this scripture and think it only applies to children. That is true of verse 1, which instructs children to obey their parents. However, verse 2 was originally spoken to adults. The word "honor" here means "to prize, that is, fix a valuation upon, to revere."[11] God expects you to honor your parents. Honor is a big deal to God—a very big deal. It doesn't matter what they've done or what you think they deserve; God requires you to honor them.

---

11 Strong's Concordance, s.v. "honor," https://biblehub.com/greek/5091.htm?utm_source=chatgpt.com.

> *"For though you might have ten thousand instructors in Christ, yet you do not have many fathers; for in Christ Jesus I have begotten you through the gospel."*
> —1 Corinthians 4:15 (NKJV)

Another reason you must honor them is that they have been your spiritual leaders. You have received the Word of God from them, and they've taught you how to hear His voice. Most likely, you would not be where you are spiritually without them. So, honor them in your heart, with your words, and with your actions.

"Pastor Andre, you have no idea what they did to me, you have no idea what happened." I get it. Some of us have horror stories. Many mistakes have been made. The truth is that you cannot change the heart or even the mind of other people. Sometimes, people are just set in their ways. When in bad situations, seek God about His victory plan for your situation and follow it. God will heal your heart and make things right for you.

The ultimate example of honor in a similar situation was David's relationship with Saul. If anyone had been wronged by his leader (in this case, not only his king but his father-in-law), it was David. Yet, notice his testimony:

> *Look, my father, at what I have in my hand. It is a piece of the hem of your robe! I cut it off, but I didn't kill you. This proves that I am not trying to harm you and that*

> *I have not sinned against you, even though you have been hunting for me to kill me.*
>
> *May the LORD judge between us. Perhaps the LORD will punish you for what you are trying to do to me, but I will never harm you.*
> —1 Samuel 24:11-12

This is why David became king, even though Saul turned his entire life upside down. Even though he had lost his wife and years of his life due to Saul's jealousy and hate. Even then, he refused to dishonor Saul. Honor matters to God. No matter what, honor them.

Having said that, you can do things to ensure that your children don't endure what you endured, should the Lord have them serve with you as well. The following is a list of things to avoid:

1) Don't use the ministry as a tool to interfere in their marriage or family life.
I've noticed that so many PKs have significant issues in their marriages. Of course, there are a plethora of reasons why people struggle in their marriages (or even go through divorce). But the fact that PKs' marriages consistently struggle points to an issue that is all too prevalent in family ministry: family interference.

> *"Therefore a man shall leave his father and mother and be joined to his wife, and they shall become one flesh."*
> —Genesis 2:24 (NKJV)

Even if your child joins you in ministry, you would be wrong to violate God's order in the home by interfering in their marriage. In fact, you should be a great blessing to their marriage.

Unfortunately, there are too many cases where the PK's family brutally mistreats the PK's spouse. Also, the PK's family may use the ministry to force the PK and his or her spouse to make life decisions for personal (not ministry) reasons. This is not lost on the spouse, and it leads to significant issues in that marriage. Just because they are your child or they serve under you in ministry doesn't mean you get to run their marriage or their life.

2) Be Humble and Kind
"Love suffers long *and* is kind; love does not envy; love does not parade itself, is not puffed up" (1 Corinthians 13:4, NKJV).

Anyone who has had success faces one of the greatest temptations of all—pride. Ministers aren't immune to this. Unfortunately, sometimes the meanest and most prideful people that you can meet are successful ministers. Because God has used them so greatly, because they have impacted so many lives, because they have been in ministry for so many years, they feel that it gives them a license to be mean and puffed up. That is unbiblical and a sign of spiritual immaturity. A number of ministry families have suffered and broken up because of this behavior. (There's a reason why Proverbs 16:18 says, "pride goes before a fall!")

> *"Now the man Moses was very humble, more than all men who were on the face of the earth."*
> —Numbers 12:3

Has anyone had the impact that Moses had? Yet, he will be known throughout eternity for his humility. Jesus described Himself as "meek and lowly in heart." That's a qualification for being a great leader. That's also a qualification for successful family ministry. It is very difficult to work for a prideful and disrespectful boss. It is even more so when that boss is your parent, especially when they use the position that God gave them as justification.

Yes, Moses had moments when he strongly corrected people. Jesus did, too. However, those moments didn't define them, nor their relationships, and it shouldn't define your children, either, should they serve with you in ministry one day.

> *"A wise man will hear and increase learning, And a man of understanding will attain wise counsel."*
> —Proverbs 1:5 (NKJV)

If God calls your children to serve with you, it's for the purpose of helping you. That means they will have a perspective and wisdom that you and your ministry will need to fully accomplish its mission. Learn from Solomon; he was the wisest man on earth but still had counselors to whom he listened.

God even had a donkey speak to a prophet! So don't be surprised if God speaks to you from time to time through your children.

ONE MISTAKE WE MAKE TOO OFTEN IN MINISTRY IS STAY MARRIED TO OUR METHODS RATHER THAN TO THE MESSAGE.

I have learned by observation that a number of ministries have successfully reached a second generation and expanded their impact by years because the leaders of those ministries truly listened to the counsel that came from the PKs God sent to help them.

3) Let Them Be Who God Called Them to Be

> *Then Saul gave David his own armor—a bronze helmet and a coat of mail. David put it on, strapped the sword over it, and took a step or two to see what it was like, for he had never worn such things before.*

> "I can't go in these," he protested to Saul. "I'm not used to them." So David took them off again. He picked up five smooth stones from a stream and put them into his shepherd's bag. Then, armed only with his shepherd's staff and sling, he started across the valley to fight the Philistine.
> —1 Samuel 17:38-40

God didn't call David to be Saul. God won't call your child to be you. Don't force your child to wear your armor and do ministry just like you! It won't work. It will not only lead to misery for them, but most importantly, it will hinder their effectiveness for the kingdom of God. If David had walked on the battlefield with Saul's armor, Goliath would not have been defeated that day, Israel would not have been victorious, and God would not have been glorified through their victory.

> "This is not a reference to David, for after David had done the will of God in his own generation, he died and was buried with his ancestors, and his body decayed."
> —Acts 13:36

One reason why God has made them different from you is that they are called to minister in their own generation. One mistake we make too often in ministry is staying married to our methods rather than to the message. Often, those methods aren't the latest thing but the old way of doing things that we are most comfortable with.

When the time comes for them to pour their new wine into new wineskins, support them. Following "your ways," as Paul called it, does not mean your children should follow your ministry methods, but the example that you've set in how you live your life. Help keep them on track with the Word of God and the Spirit of God. Encourage them to be like Jesus. Help them to be what God made them to be.

4) Don't Force Them into Ministry Assignments
"Paul, a bondservant of Jesus Christ, called to be an apostle, separated to the gospel of God" (Romans 1:1, NKJV).

It is God who calls people into ministry assignments, not people . . . not even their parents. My parents didn't "call" my sisters and me into ministry when we left high school. Although they knew that we were called, they allowed us to hear from God for ourselves and did not force us into going to ministry school.

Too often, family members fall into the same trap as the world. A man spends his life building a corner store, and now that his son is of age, he wants him to take over the store. Not only does he want it, but he pressures him to do it and ridicules him if he doesn't want to or isn't ready yet.

Let your children hear from God for themselves, like I hope you would with any ministry staff. In fact, I would be even more careful when it comes to your kids. Not handling them the right way can not only have a large impact on whether they follow God's will for their lives, but also on your relationship with them. Remember, you are not the Holy Ghost. God will never abdicate His throne and give you His place in their lives. They are God's slaves, not yours.

5) Don't Hold Them Back from God's Calling
"So after more fasting and prayer, the men laid their hands on them and sent them on their way" (Acts 13:3).

It's quite possible that God's plan for your child's life isn't the same as your plan. The time may come when you have to release them into a new assignment separate from you. When that time comes, let them go! In fact, be their biggest fan. Even if you believe that they are missing God, wholeheartedly support them while praying for them. That support will mean everything to them. If they are missing it, it will get you out of the way and allow God to speak to their heart.

> *Anoint Elisha son of Shaphat from the town of Abel-meholah to replace you as my prophet.*
> —1 Kings 19:16

Should God call them to take over your work, trust God and trust them. Every situation and process is different, so follow the Holy Spirit in it. When it's time for you to step out of the way and let them ride the bike on their own, let them. Don't be the one who rebels against what God has said, for any reason. Ultimately, it is God's ministry, not yours. Just like God knew what He was doing when He chose you, God knows what He is doing in choosing them. In fact, He may be so confident in them because He made sure that you trained them. When it comes to your children, be a servant leader who is focused on helping and releasing them into the future God has for them—be *for* them! As one well-known minister said, "Fathers are for the sons, not the sons for the fathers."

Family ministry can be a tremendous blessing to the family and to the world around them. There are so many great examples of that today. Should you be in a family ministry, walk in love, forgive, honor, heal, and train your children up in such a way that they, too, are mighty and making a difference for God in the earth!

CHAPTER 21

WHEN A LEADER FAILS

Many of the principles of the last two chapters not only apply to PKs, but also to those who are spiritual sons and daughters of ministry leaders. We are to honor our leaders, no matter what. We are to maintain a clear conscience in how we deal with them. When mistreated, we are to address our concerns and, when done wrong, we are to forgive, trusting that God will make things right.

> **NOT GOING TO CHURCH BECAUSE A MINISTER MAY FALL IS LIKE NEVER FLYING AGAIN IN A PLANE DUE TO A FEAR OF CRASHING.**

Spiritual sons and daughters aren't just ministers, but members of their churches and partners with their ministries. Recently, a number of them have faced a situation—a fallen spiritual leader—that has caused them to struggle with feelings of anger, betrayal, and more. Now, let me say that the world likes to pretend as though ministers are falling into sin all around us when, in reality, it is still a relatively rare occurrence. Thousands of planes fly safely every day, but all the attention goes to the one that crashed. Most people understand that just because there's a crash every once in a while doesn't mean that there aren't hundreds of thousands of flights that don't. The same is true for ministry leaders. Not going to church because a minister may fall is like never flying again in a plane due to a fear of crashing.

However, when it does happen, there can be significant damage to the hearts and spiritual lives of their sons and daughters. This is a major cause of church hurt for a number of people today. The question then is, how do we when a church leader falls? Let's look at a few scriptures:

Dear brothers and sisters, if another believer is overcome by some sin, you who are godly should gently and humbly help that person back onto the right path. And be careful not to fall into the same temptation yourself.
—Galatians 6:1

The first answer to our question is to respond with humility. Be careful not to spend your time attacking the individual who had a moral failure. Don't pile on! The Bible is very clear here and in other places that this could easily be you! Instead, focus on and pray for their restoration.

WHEN A LEADER FAILS

One day he drank some wine he had made, and he became drunk and lay naked inside his tent. Ham, the father of Canaan, saw that his father was naked and went outside and told his brothers. Then Shem and Japheth took a robe, held it over their shoulders, and backed into the tent to cover their father. As they did this, they looked the other way so they would not see him naked.

When Noah woke up from his stupor, he learned what Ham, his youngest son, had done.

Then he cursed Canaan, the son of Ham:

"May Canaan be cursed!

May he be the lowest of servants to his relatives."

Then Noah said,

> "May the LORD, the God of Shem, be blessed,
> and may Canaan be his servant!
> May God expand the territory of Japheth!
> May Japheth share the prosperity of Shem,
> and may Canaan be his servant."
> Noah lived another 350 years after the great flood.
> —Genesis 9:21-28

The second answer is to respond with honor. There's more in this scripture than I could teach in this chapter, but one thing we can gather is that Shem and Japheth handled Noah's failure with honor. Ham did not. The way they handled the situation had an impact not just on them but on their generations.

Notice that God hadn't given up on Noah. He still lived 350 years after. God doesn't give up on fallen leaders as easily as we do. Their next assignment may look different, but it may be even more impactful than the last. Don't jump at the opportunity to take them down or rob them of the work that God had them build because of your ambition or pride. I've seen this too often recently, and I find it appalling. I think God does, too.

> "Then the churches throughout all Judea, Galilee, and Samaria had peace and were edified. And walking in the fear of the Lord and in the comfort of the Holy Spirit, they were multiplied."
> —Acts 9:31 (NKJV)

The third answer is to ask for God's comfort. As we read earlier, 2 Corinthians 1 reveals that God has made supernatural comfort available to us for any situation that we may face. That would include this one. Let God heal you. Then get back to work helping His church multiply in the earth.

CHAPTER 22

IT'S TIME TO MOVE PAST CHURCH HURT

I know what I'm doing. I have it all planned out—plans to take care of you, not abandon you, plans to give you the future you hope for" (Jeremiah 29:11, MSG).

God has plans for you. He has crafted a future for you that is so wonderful that you will hardly believe it. A future where you will enjoy your life and make a difference in this world for him. Satan doesn't want to see that. That is why he attacked you. That is why he hurt you—to get you away from God. Don't fall for it anymore. Let God heal you, let God mature you, and let God use you to help others in this world. Never again give the enemy the pleasure of slowing you down in your pursuit of God or His plan for your life.

Join the ranks of Joseph, David, Paul, and Jesus! Instead of letting church hurt turn into church hate, turn it into a testimony of how God healed you, developed you, and used you in spite of what you went through. If you do that, your future will be bright!

ABOUT THE AUTHOR

André Butler is the pastor of Faith Xperience Church in the heart of Downtown Detroit, where he's known for his practical preaching and passion for helping people step into the future God has for them. A dynamic communicator and sought-after conference speaker, André is also an accomplished author, screenwriter, and producer. He serves as president of Faith Xperience Films and the Faith Xperience Network, with his work featured in *Jet* and *Gospel Today*, and broadcast on BET—earning two Telly Awards and the Streaming Broadcaster of the Year title. A graduate of Rhema Bible Training Center and Kennesaw State University, André resides in Metro Detroit.

ADDITIONAL RESOURCES

André's Books:

Life After: Moving from Pain to Promise
You Can Win: Slaying the Goliaths of Your Life Slayin
Find Your Y: Answers to Life's Most Important Question
In My Feelings: Overcoming Discouragement, Depression, and Grief
Bae or Nah: Finding the Love of your Life
Not in My House!
It's Gonna Be Alright
God's Future for You: See How Amazing Your Life Can Be Living Life to the Full

Follow André:

 Andre Butler Ministries: *AndreButler.com*
Faith Xperience Church: *Myfaithx.com*

 Andre Butler

 andrebutler

 iamAndreButler

 youtube.com/PastorAndreButler

www.ingramcontent.com/pod-product-compliance
Lightning Source LLC
Chambersburg PA
CBHW050904160426
43194CB00011B/2280